C++ Initialization Story

A Guide Through All Initialization Options and Related C++ Areas

Bartłomiej Filipek

C++ Initialization Story

A Guide Through All Initialization Options and Related C++ Areas

Bartłomiej Filipek

ISBN 9798371581426

© 2021 - 2023 Bartłomiej Filipek

For Wiola, Mikołaj and Feliks

Contents

About the Book i
    Why should you read this book? i
    Learning objectives i
    The structure of the book ii
    Who is this book for? iii
    Prerequisites iii
    Reader feedback & errata iii
    Example code iv
    Formatting & Layout iv

About the Author vii

Acknowledgements ix

Revision History xi

1. **Local Objects** 1
    Starting with custom type 3
    Setting values to zero 6
    Copy and direct initialization 7
    Initialization with aggregates 8
    Default data member initialization 9
    Summary 11

2. **Initialization With Constructors** 13
    Defining a class 13
    Basics of constructors 16
    Body of a constructor 25
    Adding constructors to `DataPacket` 27
    Compiler-generated default constructors 28

	Explicit constructors and conversions	31
	Difference between direct and copy initialization	34
	Implicit conversion and converting constructors	36
	Constructor summary	38
3.	**Copy and Move Operations**	**39**
	Copy constructor	39
	Move constructor	47
	Distinguishing from assignment	54
	Adding debug logging to constructors	58
	Trivial classes and user-provided default constructors	60
	Summary	64
4.	**Delegating and Inheriting Constructors**	**65**
	Delegating constructors	65
	Limitations	67
	Inheritance	68
	Inheriting constructors	71
	Summary	73
5.	**Destructors**	**75**
	Basics	75
	Objects allocated on the heap	78
	Destructors and data members	80
	Virtual destructors and polymorphism	82
	Partially created objects	85
	A compiler-generated destructor	89
	Summary	90
6.	**Type Deduction and Initialization**	**91**
	Deduction with `auto`	91
	About value categories in C++	93
	Rules for `auto` type deduction	94
	Deduction with `decltype`	97
	Printing type info	100
	Structured bindings since C++17	102
	Template Argument Deduction for Class Templates	106
	Lifetime extension, references, and loops	108
	Almost Always Auto	110

	Summary 112
7.	**Quiz from Chapters 1...6** 115
8.	**Non-Static Data Member Initialization** 119
	How it works 119
	Investigation 120
	Experiments 121
	Other forms of NSDMI 123
	Copy constructor and NSDMI 127
	Move constructor and NSDMI 129
	C++14 changes 131
	C++20 changes 131
	Limitations of NSDMI 132
	NSDMI: Advantages and Disadvantages 136
	Summary 137
9.	**Containers as Data Members** 139
	The basics 139
	Using `std::initializer_list` 142
	Example implementation 146
	The cost of copying elements 150
	Some inconvenience - non-copyable types 152
	More options (advanced) 153
	Summary 155
10.	**Non-regular Data Members** 157
	Constant non-static data members 157
	Pointers as data members 160
	Smart pointers as data members 163
	References as data members 171
	Summary 175
11.	**Non-local objects** 177
	Storage duration and linkage 177
	Initialization of non-local static objects 187
	`constinit` in C++20 189
	Static variables in a function scope 192
	About static data members 194

Motivation for inline variables	196
Global inline variables	203
`constexpr` and `inline` variables	204
Summary	205

12. Aggregates and Designated Initializers in C++20 . . . 207
Aggregates as of C++20 . . . 207
The basics of designated initializers . . . 213
Rules for designated initializers . . . 214
Advantages of designated initialization . . . 215
Examples . . . 215
Summary . . . 217

13. Techniques and Use Cases . . . 219
Using `explicit` for strong types . . . 219
Best way to initialize `string` data members . . . 223
Reducing extra copies through `emplace` and `in_place` . . . 227
The copy and swap idiom . . . 232
CRTP class counter . . . 234
Several initialization types in one class . . . 237
Meyers Singleton and C++11 . . . 241
Factory with self-registering types and static initialization . . . 242
Summary . . . 248

14. The Final Quiz And Exercises . . . 249
Exercises . . . 253

Appendix A - Rules for Special Member Function Generation . . . 259
The diagram . . . 259
Rule of zero . . . 262
Rule of three (deprecated!) . . . 262
Rule of 5 and 6 - modern C++ . . . 263
Moveable-only types . . . 264
Polymorphic base classes . . . 264

Appendix B - Quiz and Exercises Answers . . . 265

References . . . 269

Index . . . 271

About the Book

Initialization in C++ is a hot topic! The internet is full of discussions about best practices, and there are even funny memes on that subject. The situation is not surprising, as there are more than a dozen ways to initialize a simple integer value, complex rules for the auto-type deduction, data members, and object lifetime nuances.

And here comes the book.

Throughout this text, you will learn practical options to initialize various categories of variables and data members in Modern C++. More specifically, this text teaches multiple types of initialization, constructors, non-static data member initialization, inline variables, designated initializers, and more. Additionally, you'll see the changes and new techniques from C++11 to C++20 and lots of examples to round out your understanding.

The plan is to explain most (if not all) parts of initialization, learn lots of excellent C++ techniques, and see what happens under the hood.

Why should you read this book?

With Modern C++ (since C++11), we have many new features to streamline work and simplify our code. One area of improvement is initialization. Modern C++ added new initialization rules, trying to make it easy while keeping old behavior and compatibility (mainly from the C language). Sometimes the rules might seem confusing and complex, though, and even the ISO committee might need to correct some things along the way. The book will help you navigate through those principles and understand this topic better. What's more, initialization is just one aspect of this text. You'll learn all related topics around classes, constructors, destructors, object lifetime, or even how the compiler processes data at start-up.

Learning objectives

The goal is to equip you with the following knowledge:

- Explain rules about object initialization, including regular variables, data members, and non-local objects.

- How to implement special member functions (constructors, destructors, copy/move operations) and when they are helpful.
- How to efficiently initialize non-static data members using C++11 features like non-static data member initialization, inheriting, and delegating constructors.
- How to streamline working with static variables and static data members with inline variables from C++17.
- How to work with container-like members, non-copyable data members (like `const` data members) or move-able only data members, or even lambdas.
- What is an aggregate, and how to create such objects with designated initializers from C++20.

The structure of the book

The book contains 14 chapters in the following structure:

- Chapters 1 to 5 create a foundation for the rest of the book. They cover basic initialization rules, constructors, destructors, and the basics of data members.
- Chapter 6 describes type deduction that can be used to declare objects: `auto`, `decltype`, Almost Always Auto rule, structured bindings.
- Chapter 7 is a quiz with 10 questions from the first "part" of the book.
- Chapter 8 describes Non-static Data Member Initialization (NSDMI), a powerful feature from C++11 that improves how we work with data members. At the end of the chapter, you can solve a few exercises.
- Chapter 9 discusses how to initialize container-like data members.
- Chapter 10 contains information about non-regular data members and how to handle them in a class. You'll learn about `const` data members, `unique_ptr` as a data member, and references.
- Chapter 11 describes static non-local variables, static objects, various storage duration options, and `inline` variables from C++17 and `constinit` from C++20.
- Chapter 12 moves to C++20 and describes Designated Initializers, a handy feature based on similar thing from the C language.
- Chapter 13 shows various techniques like passing strings into constructors, strong typing, CRTP class counter, Copy and Swap idiom, and more.
- Chapter 14 is the final quiz with questions from the whole book.

And there are two appendices:
- Appendix A - a handy guide about rules for compiler-generated special member functions.
- Appendix B - answers to quizzes and exercises.

Who is this book for?

The book is intended for beginner/intermediate C++ programmers who want to learn various aspects of initialization in Modern C++ (from C++11 to C++20).

You should know at least some of the basics of creating and using custom classes.

This text is also helpful for experienced programmers who know older C++ standards and want to move into C++17/C++20.

Prerequisites

- You should have basic knowledge of C++ expressions and primitive types.
- You should be able to implement an elementary class with several data members. Know how to create and manipulate objects of such a class in a basic way.

Reader feedback & errata

If you spot an error, a typo, a grammar mistake, or anything else (especially logical issues!) that should be corrected, please send your feedback to bartek@cppstories.com or submit an issue at github.com/fenbf/cppinitbook_public/issues[1].

Here's the errata with the list of fixes:

www.cppstories.com/p/cppinitbook/[2]

Your feedback matters! Writing an honest review can help with the book promotion and the quality of my further work. The book has a dedicated page at GoodReads. Please share your feedback at:

C++ Initialization Story by Bartłomiej Filipek @Goodreads[3].

Or write a review at Amazon if you get this book in print form.

---

[1] https://github.com/fenbf/cppinitbook_public/issues
[2] https://www.cppstories.com/p/cppinitbook/
[3] https://www.goodreads.com/book/show/62606823-c-initialization-story

Example code

You can find source code of all examples in this separate GitHub public repository.

https://github.com/fenbf/cppinitbook_public/tree/main/examples

You can browse individual files or download the whole branch:

https://github.com/fenbf/cppinitbook_public/archive/refs/heads/main.zip

Code license

The code for the book is available under the MIT License model.

Formatting & Layout

Code samples are presented in a monospaced font, similar to the following example:

Title Of the Example

```cpp
#include <iostream>

int main() {
    const std::string text { "Hello World" };
    std::cout << text << '\n';
}
```

Or shorter snippets (without a title and sometimes `include` statements):

```cpp
int foo() {
    return std::clamp(100, 1000, 1001);
}
```

When available, you'll also see a link to online compilers where you can play with the code. For example:

Example title. Run @Compiler Explorer

```
#include <iostream>

int main() {
    std::cout << "Hello World!";
}
```

You can click on the link in the title, and then it should open the website of a given online compiler (in the above case, it's Compiler Explorer). You can compile the sample, see the output, and experiment with the code directly in your browser. Here's a basic overview of Compiler Explorer:

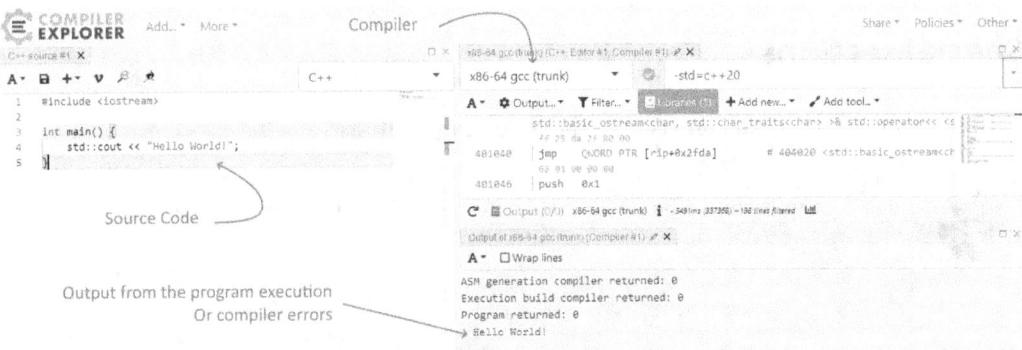

A Compiler Explorer layout used in the book

Snippets of longer programs might be shortened to present only the core mechanics. They may lack some `#include` statements or have a "compressed" line. Click on the Online Compiler link to see the full version of the program or see them in the public repository.

Recommendation for Compiler Explorer and C++ Reference

When executing the examples on Compiler Explorer, you may select a term (keyword, class, function, container or other) and then right-click (or equivalent). A context menu will appear and you can select `Search on CppReference`, which will take you to the C++ Reference documentation of the corresponding browser language, if such C++ Reference version exists[4].

---
[4]Thanks to Javier Estrada for suggesting this cool tip!

Syntax highlighting limitations

The current version of the book might show some limitations regarding syntax highlighting. For example:

- The first method of a class is not highlighted - First method of class not highlighted in C++ · Issue #791[5].
- Template method is not highlighted C++ lexer doesn't recognize function if return type is templated · Issue #1138[6].
- Modern C++ attributes are sometimes not appropriately recognized.

Other issues for C++ and Pygments: C++ Issues · github/pygments/pygments[7].

Special sections

Throughout the book, you can also see the following sections:

 This is an Information Box with extra notes related to the current section.

 This is a Warning Box with potential risks and threats related to a given topic.

> This is a Quote Box. In the book, it's often used to quote the C++ Standard.

---

[5]https://github.com/pygments/pygments/issues/791
[6]https://github.com/pygments/pygments/issues/1138
[7]https://github.com/pygments/pygments/issues?q=is%3Aissue+is%3Aopen+C%2B%2B

About the Author

Bartłomiej (Bartek) Filipek is a C++ software developer from the beautiful city of Cracow in Southern Poland. He started his professional career in 2007 and in 2010 he graduated from Jagiellonian University with a Masters Degree in Computer Science.

Bartek currently works at Xara[8], where he develops features for advanced document editors. He also has experience with desktop graphics applications, game development, large-scale systems for aviation, writing graphics drivers and even biofeedback. In the past, Bartek has also taught programming (mostly game and graphics programming courses) at local universities in Cracow.

Since 2011 Bartek has been regularly blogging at cppstories.com[9] (started as bfilipek.com[10]). The blog focuses on core C++ and getting up-to-date with the C++ Standards. He's also a co-organiser of the C++ User Group in Cracow[11]. You can hear Bartek in one @CppCast episode[12] where he talks about C++17, blogging and text processing.

Since October 2018, Bartek has been a C++ Expert for the Polish National Body which works directly with ISO/IEC JTC 1/SC 22 (C++ Standardisation Committee). Bartek was awarded his first MVP title for the years 2019/2020 by Microsoft.

In his spare time, he loves collecting and assembling Lego models with his son.

Bartek is the author of C++17 In Detail[13] and C++ Lambda Story[14].

---

[8] http://www.xara.com/
[9] https://www.cppstories.com]
[10] https://www.bfilipek.com
[11] https://www.meetup.com/C-User-Group-Cracow/
[12] http://cppcast.com/2018/04/bartlomiej-filipek/
[13] https://leanpub.com/cpp17indetail
[14] https://leanpub.com/cpplambda

Acknowledgements

This book wouldn't be possible without valuable input from many C++ experts and friends. I especially would like to thank to the following people:

- JFT (John Taylor),
- Mariusz Jaskółka,
- Florin Chertes (see his profile at LinkedIn[15]),
- Konrad Jaśkowiec (see his profile at LinkedIn[16]),
- Professor Boguslaw Cyganek (see his profile at AGH university page[17]),
- Dawid Pilarski (see his blog at panicsoftware.com[18]),
- Javier Estrada (see his blog at javierestrada.blog[19]),
- Jonathan Boccara (from fluentcpp.com[20]),
- Andreas Fertig (see his blog at andreasfertig.blog[21]),
- Peter Sommerlad (see his website and training info at sommerlad.ch[22]),
- Timur Doumler (see his website at timur.audio[23] and his Twitter[24]),
- Michael Goldshteyn, Software Architect.

They spent a lot of time on finding even little things that could be improved and extended.

Last but not least, I got a lot of valuable feedback from my blog readers, Patreon Discord Server (See C++Stories @Patreon[25]), and discussions at C++ Polska[26]. Thank you all!

With all of the help from those kind people, the book quality got better and better!

---

[15] https://www.linkedin.com/in/florin-ioan-chertes-41b6845/
[16] https://pl.linkedin.com/in/konrad-ja%C5%9Bkowiec-84585159
[17] https://home.agh.edu.pl/~cyganek/
[18] https://blog.panicsoftware.com/
[19] https://javierestrada.blog/
[20] https://www.fluentcpp.com/
[21] https://andreasfertig.blog/
[22] https://sommerlad.ch/
[23] https://timur.audio/
[24] https://twitter.com/timur_audio
[25] https://www.patreon.com/cppstories
[26] https://cpp-polska.pl/

Revision History

- 20th June 2022 - The first public version! Missing parts: some sections in 10. Containers as Data Members, some sections in 11. Non-regular Data Members.
- 22nd June 2022 - new sections on NSDMI, direct init and parens, more about inheriting constructors, link to GoodReads, wording, hotfixes.
- 24th June 2022 - updated the "copy and move constructor" chapter, typos and small wording improvements.
- 16th July 2022 - Containers as Data Members chapter rewritten, `noexcept` consistency and `noexcept` move operations advantages in the move constructor section, wording, fixes, layout.
- 13th September 2022 - changed title to "C++ Initialization Story", adapted book structure, rewritten "Non-local objects" chapter (previously only on `inline` variables), new extracted chapter on Techniques, new section on CRTP.
- 18th November 2022 - heavily updated and completed "Non-regular data members" chapter, `constinit` and `thread_local` sections in the "Non-local objects" chapter, filled the "implicit conversion" section in the Constructors chapter.
- 23rd December 2022 - content completed! Added Deduction chapter, filled missing sections in the Techniques chapter. Layout improvements, a few more questions, exercises and fixes.
- 4th February 2023 - updated layout, wording improvements, fixes, improve consistency of examples.
- 27th February 2023 - the first edition in Print!
- 13th April 2023 - the final quiz questions 6th and 8th clarification, small layout fixes.
- 19th June 2023 - a batch of minor fixes and clarifications based on user feedback.

1. Local Objects

Let's start simple and ask, "what is initialization?" When we go to the definition from C++Reference[1], we can read:

> *Initialization* of a variable provides its initial value at the time of construction.

We can translate this definition to the following example:

```cpp
void foo() {
    int x = 42;
    // ... use 'x' later...
}
```

Above, we have a function with a local variable x. The variable is declared as integer and initialized with the value 42. This is one of many ways you can assign that initial value. Here are some more options:

```cpp
struct Point { int x; int y; };            // declare a custom type
Point createPoint(int x) { return {x, -x}; }
int main() {
    int x { 42 };                          // list initialization
    double y = { 100.0 };                  // copy list initialization
    auto f = 90.5f;                        // auto type deduction
    auto z = createPoint(42);              // through a factory function
    std::string s (10, 'x');               // calling a constructor
    Point p { 10 };                        // aggregate initialization
    std::array<float, 100> numbers { 1.1f, 2.2f }; // list initialization
    // ...
}
```

---

[1] https://en.cppreference.com/w/cpp/language/initialization

The list of options is not complete, and we can also extend the syntax on class data members, `static` variables, thread locals, or even dynamic memory allocations.

In theory, initialization is simple: "put a value into a memory location of a newly created variable". However, such action relates to many parts of application code (local vs. non-local scope vs. thread) and various places in the memory (like stack vs. heap). That's why the syntax or the behavior might be slightly different.

In C++, we have at least the following forms of initialization:

- aggregate initialization
- constant initialization
- default initialization
- direct initialization
- copy initialization
- list initialization
- reference initialization
- value initialization
- zero initialization
- plus related topics like copy elision, static variables, conversion sequences, constructors, assignment, dynamic memory, storage, and more.

While the list sounds complex, we'll move through those topics step by step revealing core concepts. Later we'll address more advanced examples and see what happens inside the C++ machinery.

While we can explain most cases on integers and other numerical types, it's best to work on something more practical. The book starts with some elementary custom types, then considers various issues we might have with their early implementations. Later the types will expand, giving us more context and compelling use cases.

Declaration vs definition

To be precise, let's address the difference between a definition and a declaration in C++.

> *Declaration* introduces a name to the compiler, while *definition* "implements" or instantiates this name/entity.

For example, you can have many declarations of a function but only a single definition (implementation). Similarly, you can declare a global variable in many translation units, but there must be only one definition of it in one place. For variables, a definition means allocating some storage for the object.

```
extern int x;             // declaration only
int y;                    // definition (and default initialization)
std::string str { "Hi" }; // definition and direct initialization
```

See more in the C++ Standard basic.def[2] section.

Starting with custom type

Defining a class or a struct (a custom or user-defined type) in C++ allows you to model your problem domain and solve problems more naturally. Rather than working with a bunch of variables and functions, it's best to group them and provide a consistent API (Application Programming Interface). C++ provides a set of built-in types, including boolean, integral, character, and floating-point. Additionally, you can use objects from the Standard Library, like various collections, `std::string`, `std::vector`, `std::map`, `std::set`, and many others. You can collect these essential components and build your types.

To create a background for our main topic, let's start with a type representing Car Information for a car listing app. A system reads the car/truck information from a database and displays it in the application. For an easy start, the type holds four members: name (a `std::string`), production year, number of seats, and engine power.

---

[2]https://timsong-cpp.github.io/cppwp/n4868/basic.def#1

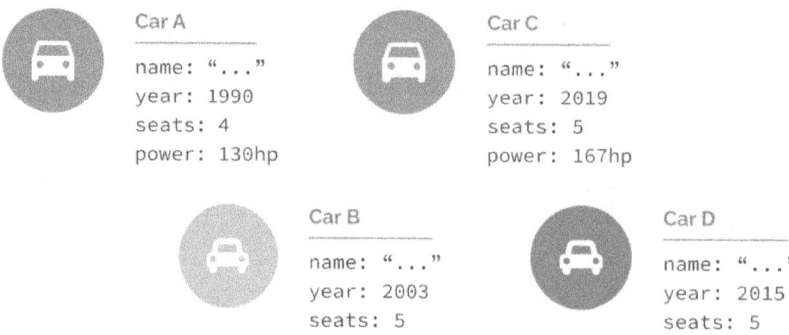

Below there's the first version of the code for that `CarInfo` type:

Ex 1.1. Simple `CarInfo` structure. Run @Compiler Explorer

```cpp
#include <iostream>
#include <string>

struct CarInfo {
    std::string name;
    unsigned year;
    unsigned seats;
    double power;
};

int main() {
    CarInfo firstCar;
    firstCar.name = "Renault Megane";
    firstCar.year = 2003;
    firstCar.seats = 5;
    firstCar.power = 116;
    std::cout << "name: " << firstCar.name << '\n';
    std::cout << "year: " << firstCar.year << '\n';
    std::cout << "seats: " << firstCar.seats << '\n';
    std::cout << "power (hp): " << firstCar.power << '\n';
}
```

In the above example, we defined a simple structure that holds data for a `CarInfo`. This structure is also called "user-defined" as it's not a built-in type (like an `int` or `double`). The code is super simple, contains some issues, and follows the style of C++03. In the following few chapters, I'll guide you through the code and help you understand the problems and how to eliminate them. We'll also modernize it to include the latest C++ (up to C++20) features.

First: `name`, `year`, `seats`, and `power` are called *non-static data members*. Each instance of the `CarInfo` class has its own set of those members. In other words, we group variables to create a representation for models in our problem domain. A user-defined type might also have *static data members*, which are data shared between all instances of a given type. For example, we could imagine a *static* member variable called `numAllCars` that would indicate the total number of cars created in our program. We'll talk about *static data members* later in chapter 11 Static Variables.

Now, let's investigate the code in detail. The definition and the declaration of the variable `firstCar` in the `main()` function:

```
CarInfo firstCar;
```

It is called *default initialization* and, for our `struct`, it will leave all data members of built-in types with *indeterminate values*. Similarly, you can get the same effect for simple types when declared in function (as such variables have automatic storage duration)[3]:

```
void foo() {
    int i;       // indeterminate value!
    double d;    // indeterminate value!
}
```

Please note that reading from an indeterminate value is **Undefined Behaviour** and might lead to all kinds of bugs in your code. As of late 2022, some reports mention that even 10% of exploits against security-relevant codebases are related to uninitialized variables! You can read more in a possible C++26 feature proposal: P2723: Zero-initialize objects of automatic storage duration[4]. But as of now (C++23 and before), please always initialize your variables!

The `std::string` data member `name`, on the other hand, will have an empty state (an empty string) because its default constructor will be called. More on that later.

---

[3] In contrast, `static` and thread-local objects will be zero-initialized.
[4] https://wg21.link/P2723

Once the object is created and uninitialized, we can access its members and set proper values. By default, `struct` has public access to its members (and `class` has private access). This way, we can access and change their values directly.

What is "Automatic Storage Duration"?

All objects in a program have four possible ways to be "stored": automatic, static, thread, or dynamic. Automatic means that the storage is allocated at the start of the scope, like in a function. Most local variables have automatic storage duration (except those declared as `static`, `extern`, or `thread_local`). We'll discuss this more in the chapter on non-local objects.

Setting values to zero

You might feel very worried that after creating a `CarInfo` object, most data members have some indeterminate values (leading to Undefined Behaviour and security issues!). We can fix this and make sure the data is at least set to "zero". Have a look:

Ex 1.2. Value initialization for the `CarInfo` structure. Run @Compiler Explorer

```
CarInfo emptyCar{};
std::cout << "name: " << emptyCar.name << '\n';
std::cout << "year: " << emptyCar.year << '\n';
std::cout << "seats: " << emptyCar.seats << '\n';
std::cout << "power (hp): " << emptyCar.power << '\n';
```

The output:

```
name:
year: 0
seats: 0
power (hp): 0
```

The initialization with empty braces {} is called *value initialization* and, by default (for built-in types and classes with default constructors that are neither user-provided nor deleted), sets data to "zero" (adapted for different types). This is similar to declaring and defining the following variables:

```cpp
int i{};        // i == 0
double d{};     // d == 0.0
std::string s{}; // s is an empty string

int j = {}; // other form of value initialization
std::string str = {}; // ...
```

This time the storage duration doesn't matter, and value initialization works the same for static, dynamic, thread-local, or automatic variables. For types with default constructors (more on that later), the code will call them and, in the case of `string s;` will initialize it to an empty string.

Copy and direct initialization

Value initialization is not the only option to set some initial state. We can use more natural ways to set zero (or different values):

Using a *copy* initialization syntax:

```cpp
int i = 0;
double d = 0.55;
std::string s = "Hello World";
```

Or *direct initialization*:

```cpp
int i { 0 };
double d { 0.55 };
std::string { "Hello World" };
```

Note that *copy initialization* syntax is very common in other programming languages, so it can be very natural to use. We'll discuss the differences between those approaches in the "difference between copy and direct" section in the next chapter.

On the other hand, the `CarInfo` structure is a package of other variables, and to set them all at once, we can leverage aggregate initialization; see further.

Initialization with aggregates

Our structure has only public members, no constructors, no virtual functions, and no base classes. It fully matches the definition of an *aggregate*. C++ has special rules for such types where we can initialize their internal values with so-called *aggregate initialization*. We can use such syntax also for arrays. Here are some basic examples:

Ex 1.3. Aggregate Initialization basic syntax. Run @Compiler Explorer

```
// arrays:
int arr[] { 1, 2, 3, 4 };
float numbers[] = { 0.1f, 1.1f, 2.2f, 3.f, 4.f, 5.f };
int nums[10] { 1 }; // 1, and then all 0s

// structures:
struct Point { int x; int y; };
struct Line { Point p1; Point p2; };
Line longLine {0, 0, 100, 100 };
Line anotherLine = { 100 }; // rest set to 0
Line shortLine {{ -10, -10 }, { 10, 10 } }; // nested
```

In summary, for the above code, for local objects:

- Each array element, or non-static class member, in order of array subscript/appearance in the class definition, is copy-initialized from the corresponding clause of the initializer list.
- You can use list initialization for arrays; when the number of elements is not provided, the compiler will deduce the count (not for member variable initialization, though, see later in the Container chapter).
- If you pass fewer elements in the initializer list than the number of elements in the array, the remaining elements will be value initialized. For built-in types, it means the value of zero.
- If you provide fewer values than the number of data members in the aggregate, then the remaining data members (in the declaration order) will be effectively value initialized.

For our structure, we can write the following test code:

Ex 1.4. Aggregate initialization for the `CarInfo` structure. Run @Compiler Explorer

```cpp
struct CarInfo {
    std::string name;
    unsigned year;
    unsigned seats;
    double power;
};

void printInfo(const CarInfo& c) {
    std::cout << c.name << ", "
              << c.year << " year, "
              << c.seats << " seats, "
              << c.power << " hp\n";
}

int main() {
    CarInfo firstCar{"Megane", 2003, 5, 116 };
    printInfo(firstCar);
    CarInfo partial{"unknown"};
    printInfo(partial);
    CarInfo largeCar{"large car", 1975, 10};
    printInfo(largeCar);
}
```

This will output:

```
Megane, 2003 year, 5 seats, 116 hp
unknown, 0 year, 0 seats, 0 hp
large car, 1975 year, 10 seats, 0 hp
```

We'll discuss aggregates in further parts of the book (and see the full definition of that category of types). See a dedicated chapter about Aggregates and Designated Initialization in C++20.

Default data member initialization

What if you want to provide some default value for your data member? With value initialization, you can get zeros for various types, but sometimes it might not be good enough.

Since C++14, we can leverage *Non-static Data Member Initializers* (NSDMI), also called Default Member Initializers, to provide default values for aggregates. Have a look:

Ex 1.5. Default member initialization and aggregates. Run @Compiler Explorer

```cpp
#include <iostream>
#include <string>

struct CarInfo {
    std::string name { "unknown" };
    unsigned year { 1920 }; // direct initialization
    unsigned seats = 4;     // copy initialization
    double power { 100. };
};

void printInfo(const CarInfo& c) { /* */ }

int main() {
    CarInfo unknown;
    printInfo(unknown);
    CarInfo zeroed{};
    printInfo(zeroed);
    CarInfo partial{"large car", 1975};
    printInfo(partial);
}
```

This will print:

```
unknown, 1920 year, 4 seats, 100 hp
unknown, 1920 year, 4 seats, 100 hp
large car, 1975 year, 4 seats, 100 hp
```

The syntax is quite intuitive; you can initialize a data member at the place where it's declared. What's more various options are available, like a copy or direct initialization. As stressed before, setting some initial value can prevent undefined behavior bugs where your data has some indeterminate value. As you can see from the example, even if you use default initialization or value initialization (on the whole `CarInfo` object), data members will get values that were provided in the `struct` declaration. If you give fewer values in the aggregate initializer, the remaining members will get their defaults from the declaration.

Technically, in-class member initializers have been available since C++11, but aggregate types weren't supported initially. In this section, we've only scratched the surface of this handy technique. See the dedicated chapter for this topic: Non-static data member initialization chapter.

Summary

In this chapter, we covered some simple custom types and looked at ways to initialize their data members. We went from objects with indeterminate values to zero initialization, and then we learned about aggregates and techniques to provide default values.

Things to keep in mind:

- Default initialization for objects and variables yields indeterminate values for built-in types or default-initialize complex types (like `std::string` and set it to an empty string).
- It's essential to ensure variables are always initialized, as accessing an indeterminate value is an Undefined Behaviour and leads to severe bugs.
- Value initialization like `int x{};` for built-in types effectively yields zero initialization for them so that they will be zero (in their type).
- With value initialization `CarInfo car{};` all data members will be zero-initialized (for built-in types) or default initialized for complex types.
- *Direct initialization* like `int x { 10 };` and *copy initialization*: `int y = 100;` allows setting any value.
- Aggregates are simple types or arrays with all public data members; we can initialize them with an aggregate initialization syntax.
- Thanks to the in-class member initializer feature, you can provide default values for your data members.

What's next?

While simple types are handy, we often need to build large objects where data members depend on each other or the whole class has some invariants. In such cases, it's best to hide them behind member functions and give access to them under certain conditions. In the next chapter, we'll look at classes and **constructors**. We'll also expand the knowledge that we got so far.

2. Initialization With Constructors

In the previous chapter, you saw that C++ might treat structures with all public data members as an aggregate class. Still, aggregates are insufficient if we want better data encapsulation and a more complex class API. For full flexibility in C++, we can leverage constructors that are special member functions invoked when an object is created.

Defining a class

As a background example, let's create a type that will hold some network data. To complicate things, we'd like to compute a checksum for the data part. This computation might be handy for checking if the data was transferred correctly across the Internet (read more @Wikipedia[1]).

Ex 2.1. **DataPacket** class. Run @Compiler Explorer

```cpp
size_t calcCheckSum(const std::string& s) {
    return std::accumulate(s.begin(), s.end(), 0uz);
}
class DataPacket {
    std::string data_;
    size_t checkSum_;
    size_t serverId_;
public:
    const std::string& getData() const { return data_; }
    void setData(const std::string& data) {
        data_ = data;
        checkSum_ = calcCheckSum(data);
    }
    size_t getCheckSum() const { return checkSum_; }
    size_t getServerId() const { return serverId_; }
    void setServerId(size_t serverId) { serverId_ = serverId; }
};
```

[1] https://en.wikipedia.org/wiki/Checksum

The class above contains three *non-static data members*: `data_`, `checkSum_`, and `serverId_`. I'm using the underscore suffix to indicate private data members, a common practice in many codebases. See Google C++ Style Guide[2].

To keep things simple, I implemented the `calcCheckSum` function in terms of `std::accumulate()`, which is an algorithm from the C++ Standard Library. This code starts from `0` and adds numerical values of letters from the input `std::string`. Since C++23, we can use the `0UZ` integer literal to represent a value of `size_t` so that it matches with the return type for the function; alternatively, we could use `static_cast<size_t>` or `UL/ULL` for 32/64-bit systems respectively. For example, for `"HELLO"`, we'll get the following computations:

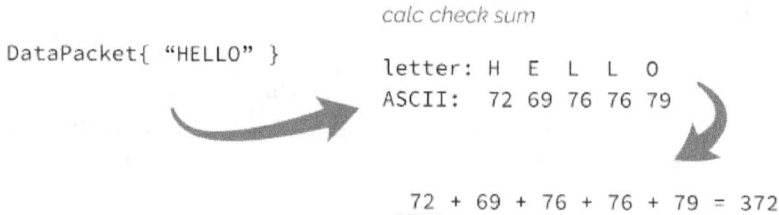

Calculating simple checksum for a string

`DataPacket` has so-called *getters* and *setters*, functions that return or change a particular data member. For example, `getData()` returns the `data_` data member, while `setData(...)` allows us to change it.

One important topic is that getters usually have `const` applied at the end. This means that a given member function is constant and cannot change the value of the members (unless they are `mutable`). If you have a `const` object, you can only call its `const` member functions. Applying `const` might improve program design as it's usually easier to reason about the state of `const` instances. For more information, see this C++ Core Guideline: Con.2: By default, make member functions const[3].

 Member functions might also have `noexcept` specifier applied. However, this topic is outside the scope of the book and won't be covered. You can find more @C++Reference - noexcept specifier[4].

---

[2]https://google.github.io/styleguide/cppguide.html#Variable_Names
[3]https://isocpp.github.io/CppCoreGuidelines/CppCoreGuidelines#con2-by-default-make-member-functions-const
[4]https://en.cppreference.com/w/cpp/language/noexcept_spec

Here's the continuation of the example where we create and use the object of the `DataPacket` class:

Ex 2.1. Simple `DataPacket` class, continuation. Run @Compiler Explorer

```
int main() {
    DataPacket packet;
    packet.setData("Programming World");
    std::cout << packet.getCheckSum() << '\n';
}
```

The code doesn't access data members directly but calls member functions to operate on the object and change its properties.

You can notice the `public` and `private` parts in the class declaration. The order of those sections is just a coding convention, and they group elements together based on their *access modifier*. In short, a member under the `public` keyword can be accessed from the outside (like calling a member function or accessing a data member). On the other hand, members under the `private` section cannot be accessed from outside[5]. In C++, you can also add `protected` to your class declaration, which means that member functions or fields are not accessible outside, but they are accessible to all inherited classes (assuming `public` inheritance, see more on that in the inheritance section further in the book).

For example, in the `main()` function above, I cannot write:

```
DataPacket packet;
packet.serverId_ = 10; // error: 'size_t DataPacket::serverId_' is private...
```

> The only difference between `class` and `struct` in C++ is that `class` has `private` as the default access modifier and `private` inheritance, while `struct` has both specified as `public`. Some C++ guidelines, for example, Google Style Guide see this link[6], suggest using `struct` only for smaller, "passive" types, with only public data members. The C++ Core Guidelines also recommend using `class` if any member is not public; see C++ Core Guidelines - C.8[7].

Since our class doesn't have any user-defined constructors (more on them in the next section), we can also use value initialization syntax to set values to zero or default values:

---

[5]Unless accessed by `friend` functions or classes.
[6]https://google.github.io/styleguide/cppguide.html#Structs_vs._Classes
[7]https://isocpp.github.io/CppCoreGuidelines/CppCoreGuidelines#c8-use-class-rather-than-struct-if-any-member-is-non-public

Ex 2.2. Value initialization for the `DataPacket` class. Run @Compiler Explorer

```cpp
int main() {
    DataPacket packet{};
    std::cout << "data: " << packet.getData() << '\n';
    std::cout << "checkSum: " << packet.getCheckSum() << '\n';
    std::cout << "serverId: " << packet.getServerId() << '\n';
}
```

This will generate the following output:

```
data:
checkSum: 0
serverId: 0
```

Because we moved data members to the private section, the class is **not an aggregate**. That's why we cannot use aggregate initialization to set all values at once. To fix this, we need to look at constructors. And that is the plan for further sections.

Basics of constructors

A constructor is a special member function that does not have a name, but we declare/define it using the enclosing class name. You cannot invoke a constructor like other member functions. Instead, the compiler calls it when an object is being initialized. It has the following syntax:

```cpp
class ClassName : public BaseClass
{
    explicit ClassName(parameter-list) = default/delete
        : base-class-initializer
        , member-init
    {
    }
};
```

- *or* **struct** — applies to `class ClassName`
- *optional* **explicit** — applies to `explicit`
- *optional base class* — applies to `: public BaseClass`
- *regular function parameter list* — applies to `(parameter-list)`
- *optional* **default/delete** — applies to `= default/delete`
- *optional, explicit calls to base class constructors* — applies to `: base-class-initializer`
- *optional, list of data member with their initializers* — applies to `, member-init`
- *regular function body* — applies to `{ }`

A constructor has the following parts:

- constructor has no name, but we define it using the name of the class,
- optional `explicit` - keyword to block implicit conversions on a given class type,
- `ClassName` - the name of the given class type (they have to match),
- `parameter-list` - a list of parameters, as in a regular function, might be empty,
- optional `= default`/`=delete` specifies if a constructor should be `deleted` (not present) or defaulted by the compiler,
- `:` - indicates the start of the member/base initialization list, required when `base-class-initializer` or `member-init` lists are present,
- optional `base-class-initializer` - a list of base classes' constructors that we explicitly want to call,
- optional `member-init` - a list of data members where we can directly initialize them,
- `{/*body*/}` - a function body.

> You can also apply `noexcept`, `[[attributes]]`, `constexpr`, and `consteval` on a constructor, but the full explanation of those additional properties goes beyond the scope of the book. Read more at C++Reference - Constructors and member initializer lists[8].

For illustrative purposes, you can find a simple class type with two data members below. The `Product` class will serve as a toy example, and then we'll apply the knowledge to the `DataPacket` class I plan to update. Let's have a look at one snippet:

```cpp
class Product {
public:
    Product() : id_{-1}, name_{"none"} { } // a default constructor
    explicit Product(int id, const std::string& name)
        : id_{id}, name_{name} { }
private:
    int id_;
    std::string name_;
};
```

The above example shows a class with two constructors. The first is called a *default constructor* and has no arguments. The second one takes two arguments. As you can notice,

---
[8]https://en.cppreference.com/w/cpp/language/constructor

C++ allows multiple constructors that look like overloaded functions (they differ by the number or types of arguments). Each constructor also has a regular function body where you can execute some code; in our case, they are both empty for now. I also applied the `explicit` keyword on the second constructor; we'll talk about it later in the `explicit` constructors section.

The primary function of constructors is to perform some actions at the start of a lifetime of an object. Usually, it means data member initialization, resource allocation (opening a file, a socket, memory allocation), or even doing some special logic (like logging).

In our case, constructors touch only data members inside a special section of constructors called *member initializer list*: like, `id_{-1}`, `name_{"none"}`. Inside this initializer list, we can also call constructors of base classes (if any). Later, we'll address inheritance in the Inheritance section.

In Modern C++ we can improve the code immediately and use *default data member initialization* that you saw in the previous chapter:

```cpp
class Product {
public:
    Product() { } // or = default
    explicit Product(int id, const std::string& name)
        : id_{id}, name_{name} { }
private:
    int id_ { -1 };
    std::string name_ { "none" };
};
```

In the above version we can set member variables in the place where they are declared, and have our default constructor shorter. The default initializer will be invoked unless there's an member initializer in a constuctor for that same member. For example in a case of the second constructor, the default initializer is not called because members are set from parameters: `id_{id}` for example. We'll explorer more cases in the Non-static Data Member Initialization chapter.

The *member initializer list* is more efficient than using the body of a constructor. Sometimes it's even the only option to initialize the value, as with types that are not assignable. See the following and *wrong* alternative:

```cpp
class Product {
public:
    Product(int paramId, const std::string& paramName)
    { id_ = paramId; name_ = paramName; } // bad code, only for illustration
private:
    int id_;
    std::string name_;
};
```

The code will yield the same values for data members as in the previous example, but the data members are set in two steps rather than one. With the *member initializer list*, data members are set directly, same as calling: `int id_ { paramId}` or `std::string name_ { paramName }`. On the other hand, if we use assignment in the constructor body, it requires two steps:

```cpp
// step 1: default init:
int id_; // indeterminate value!
std::string name_; // default ctor called
// step 2: assignment:
id_ = paramId;
name_ = paramName;
```

While this might not be a big issue for built-in simple types like `int`, you'll need some more CPU cycles for larger objects like `strings`. Please don't write such code and aim for a member initializer list to initialize your data members efficiently.

There's also one important aspect about the *initializer list*: the order of initialization. This is covered in The C++ Specification: 11.10.3 Classes[9]:

> Non-static data members are initialized in the order they were declared in the class definition (regardless of the order of the mem-initializers).

When I write the constructor in the following way:

---

[9]https://timsong-cpp.github.io/cppwp/n4868/class.base.init#13.3

```
Product() : name_{name}, id_{id} { }
```

The values will be set correctly, but the order will differ from what we think. Here's the warning from GCC compiled with -Wall option (experiment @Compiler Explorer[10]):

```
In constructor 'Product::Product()':
warning: 'Product::name_' will be initialized after [-Wreorder] ...
warning: 'int Product::id_' [-Wreorder] ...
```

The initialization order might be critical when you imply some dependency on the values. For example, we can write the following artificial sample:

```
struct S {
    int x;
    int y;
    int z;
    S(): x{0}, y{1}, z{x+y} { }
    // S(): y{0}, z{0}, x{z+y}, { }
};
```

In the above example, the first constructor initializes x and y and then uses those values to initialize z. This is complicated and might be hard to read, but it works correctly. On the other hand, in the second (commented out) constructor, the order of initialization will create undefined behavior for initializing x, as z and y will have indeterminate values. It's critical to avoid such dependencies and making sure members are initialized (for example through default data member initialization) to minimize the risk of bugs.

Let's see how a constructor works by creating some objects of the Product class:

```
Product none;
```

In the first example, we created the none object, which is default constructed. The compiler will call our default constructor; thus, the data members will be initialized to id_ = -1 and name_ = "none".

---

[10]https://godbolt.org/z/fzq9chfdG

```cpp
Product car(10, "car");
```

The example uses the form of *direct initialization*, which calls the constructor with two arguments. After the call, data members will be: `id_` = 10 and `name_` = "car".

And the last example:

```cpp
Product tvSet{ 100, "tv set" };
```

This time we also called a constructor with two arguments, but the syntax is called *direct list initialization*. Please notice that I also used this form of initialization inside the *initializer list* in constructors.

Here's the complete example:

Ex 2.3. Constructors for the Product class. Run @Compiler Explorer

```cpp
#include <iostream>
#include <string>

class Product {
public:
    Product() { }
    explicit Product(int id, const std::string& name)
        : id_{id}, name_{name} { }

    int id() const { return id_; }
    const std::string& name() const { return name_; }
private:
    int id_ { -1 };
    std::string name_ { "none" };
};

int main() {
    Product none;
    std::cout << none.id() << ", " << none.name() << '\n';

    Product car(10, "super car");
    std::cout << car.id() << ", " << car.name() << '\n';
```

```
    Product tvSet{77, "tv set" };
    std::cout << tvSet.id() << ", " << tvSet.name() << '\n';
}
```

You might also scratch your head and ask why I declared the `name` parameter as `const std::string&` rather than just `std::string&`. First, we don't want to modify this parameter in the constructor's body. What's more, `const T&` - const references can bind to "temporary" objects[11] like a string literal `"super car"`. Without a const reference, we would have to pass some named `string` object. Alternatively, we can pass the name by value and perform a "move operation" on that argument. Further in the book, I'll address this topic in detail; see chapter: A Use Case - Best Way to Initialize string Data Members.

More on uniform initialization

The syntax with curly braces "{}" is, in fact, a powerful feature of C++11 called *list initialization*, also called unofficially "uniform" or "brace" initialization. The primary motivation was to create a uniform way to initialize data and avoid some issues.

For example, because of the C++ language grammar rules, the following line won't compile:

Ex 2.4. The Most Vexing Parse Rule. Run @Compiler Explorer

```
struct Box { };
struct Product {
    Product() { }
    Product(const Box&) { }
    std::string name {"default product"};
};

int main() {
    Product p();           // << 1.
    std::cout << p.name;
    Product p2(Box());     // << 2.
    std::cout << p2.name;
}
```

The line `Product p();` looks innocent, and one could expect a default constructor to be called. Unfortunately, the compiler recognizes it as a declaration of a function! There's a C++

---

[11] The lifetime of a temporary will be extended because it's bound to a constant reference, so we won't have a dangling reference.

rule called *"most vexing parse"* which says that anything that can be parsed as a declaration must be interpreted as one. In our context, the line might mean a local function of a name p returning Product and taking no arguments. Similarly, the line with p2 also causes errors. This time the compiler thinks we declare a local function p2 returning a Product and taking Box as an argument (Box() is treated as Box(*)(), which is a function declaration called Box that takes no arguments and returns void).

But fortunately, we have at least two ways of fixing it:

```
Product p{};
Product p1;
Product p2{Box()};
Product p3{Box{}};
```

It works as expected, and the list initialization syntax is the most consistent option. Try to modify the example @Compiler Explorer[12] and fix the code. Here's a good article if you want to know more about this rule: The Most Vexing Parse: How to Spot It …@Fluent C++[13].

List initialization also handles multiple arguments and can be used inside *initializer lists*:

Ex 2.5. Multiple arguments and braces. Run @Compiler Explorer

```
struct Product {
    Product() { }
    Product(char a, char b, char c, double v)
        : name{a, b, c}, value{v} { }

    std::string name {"default product"};
    double value { 0 };
};

int main() {
    Product def{};
    std::cout << def.name << ", " << def.value << '\n';
    Product p{'x', 'y', 'z', 100.0};
    std::cout << p.name << ", " << p.value;
}
```

---

[12] https://godbolt.org/z/eo1a4T5sb
[13] https://www.fluentcpp.com/2018/01/30/most-vexing-parse/

In the above example, we not only used list initialization to call the `Product` constructor with four arguments, but we also used it to initialize the `name` and `value` data members. What's more, the curly list initialization has the following advantages:

- the syntax is similar to aggregate initialization,
- adds a way to initialize containers with a list of values at once,
- allowing checks for narrowing conversions. `int v{1.3}` won't compile and reports a narrowing error, while `int v(1.3)` works and might produce an unwanted result.

There are some annoyances with list initialization, though. For example:

```
std::vector<int> vec1 { 1, 2 }; // holds two values, 1 and 2
std::vector<int> vec2 ( 1, 2 ); // holds one value, 2!
```

Above you can see a very similar declaration of vectors, but when used with list initialization, you end up with a different vector than when using direct initialization. The list version calls a special constructor taking `std::initializer_list<int>`, while the second calls a constructor taking (`size_type count, const int& value = int()`).

Additionally, for `auto` type deduction in C++14:

```
auto i = 42;   // i is an int with value 42
auto j(42);    // j is an int with value 42
auto k{42};    // k is a std::initializer_list<int> until C++17!
```

Fortunately, this "inconsistency" was fixed in C++17, and now `auto k{42}` deduces an `int`. See more C++17 in details: fixes and deprecation @C++ Stories[14].

C++ Core Guidelines[15] suggest this way of initialization, see:

> **ES.23: Prefer the {}-initializer syntax**. The rules for {} initialization are simpler, more general, less ambiguous, and safer than for other initialization forms. Use = only when you are sure there can be no narrowing conversions. For built-in arithmetic types, use = only with `auto`. Avoid () initialization, which allows parsing ambiguities.

The guideline also mentions some exceptions:

---

[14]https://www.cppstories.com/2017/05/cpp17-details-fixes-deprecation/#new-auto-rules-for-direct-list-initialization
[15]https://isocpp.github.io/CppCoreGuidelines/CppCoreGuidelines#es23-prefer-the--initializer-syntax

> **Exception**: For containers, there is a tradition for using {...} for a list of elements and (...) for sizes: `vector<int> v(10); // 10 elements with the default value 0`
>
> `vector<int> v2{10}; // vector of 1 element with the value 10`

I'll use {} in this book for variable initialization and mention exceptions if needed.

Body of a constructor

After the member initializer list, each constructor has a regular function body, { ... }, where you can perform additional steps to modify variables or call other functions. The only difference between a regular function and a constructor is that a constructor cannot return any values. Typically, a constructor throws an exception to report an error.

Here's a small example that shows how to add some logging into a constructor body and throw an exception on error:

Ex 2.6. Logging in a constructor. Run @Compiler Explorer

```cpp
#include <iostream>
#include <stdexcept> // for std::invalid_argument

constexpr int LOWEST_ID_VALUE = -100;

class Product {
public:
    explicit Product(int id, const std::string& name)
        : id_{id}, name_{name} {
        std::cout << "Product(): " << id_ << ", " << name_ << '\n';
        if (id_ < LOWEST_ID_VALUE)
            throw std::invalid_argument{"id lower than LOWEST_ID_VALUE!"};
    }
    const std::string& name() const { return name_; }
private:
    int id_;
    std::string name_;
};
```

```
int main() {
    try {
        Product car(10, "car");
        std::cout << car.name() << " created\n";
        Product box(-101, "box");
        std::cout << box.name() << " created\n";
    }
    catch (const std::exception& ex) {
        std::cout << "Error - " << ex.what() << '\n';
    }
}
```

The above example shows a constructor that performs logging and basic parameter checking. It uses a `LOWEST_ID_VALUE`, a global constant marked with the `constexpr` keyword (the second time we used this keyword).

> The `constexpr` specifier has been available since C++11 and guarantees that a value is available at compile time for *constant expressions*. For example, you can use such a variable to set the number of elements in a C-style array. It's often perceived as a "type-safe macro definition". The keyword applies to all built-in trivial types like integral values, floating-point, or even character literals (in C++20, `std::string` might be used in the `constexpr` context but not for variables available at runtime); there's also a way to declare custom `constexpr`-ready types. You can also create a function to be `constexpr` and possibly evaluate it at compile-time; however, we won't cover such functions in this book. See more at C++Reference - constexpr[16].

If you run this program, you can see the following output:

```
Product(): 10, car
car created
Product(): -101, box
Error - id cannot be lower than LOWEST_ID_VALUE!
```

Please notice that while two constructors were called, we can see that only the first one succeeded. Since the constructor for `box` threw an exception, this object is not treated as fully created. More on that later when we'll talk about destructors.

---

[16]https://en.cppreference.com/w/cpp/language/constexpr

Adding constructors to `DataPacket`

After the introduction, we can start adding constructors to our `DataPacket` class.

Ex 2.7. Adding constructors. Run @Compiler Explorer

```cpp
class DataPacket {
    std::string data_;
    size_t checkSum_ { 0 };
    size_t serverId_ { 0 };
public:
    DataPacket() { }
    explicit DataPacket(const std::string& data, size_t serverId)
        : data_{data}, checkSum_{calcCheckSum(data)}, serverId_{serverId}
    { }

    const std::string& getData() const { return data_; }
    size_t getCheckSum() const { return checkSum_; }
    size_t getServerId() const { return serverId_; }
};
```

And here's the demo code that creates some objects:

Ex 2.7. Adding constructors, Demo. Run @Compiler Explorer

```cpp
void printInfo(const DataPacket& packet) {
    std::cout << "data: " << packet.getData() << '\n';
    std::cout << "checkSum: " << packet.getCheckSum() << '\n';
    std::cout << "serverId: " << packet.getServerId() << '\n';
}

int main() {
    DataPacket empty;
    printInfo(empty);
    DataPacket zeroed{};
    printInfo(zeroed);
    DataPacket packet{"Hello World", 101};
    printInfo(packet);
    DataPacket reply{"Hi, how are you?", 404};
```

```
    printInfo(reply);
}
```

The output:

```
data:
checkSum: 0
serverId: 0
data:
checkSum: 0
serverId: 0
data: Hello World
checkSum: 1052
serverId: 101
data: Hi, how are you?
checkSum: 1375
serverId: 404
```

In the above example, we used two constructors:

- The first is a default constructor and initializes data members to default values. It will be called for default and value initialization.
- The second constructor takes several arguments and matches them with data members. This constructor makes it easy to pass parameters all at once (previously, we needed to call setters). This one takes two parameters, but we can initialize as many data members as we need. For example, the constructors ensure the `checkSum_` variable matches `data_`. Since those two members are related, thanks to constructors and the `setData` member function, we keep the relation safe.

We can also use default member initializers inside a class, but we'll address that in detail in a separate chapter.

Compiler-generated default constructors

While C++ allows you to implement various constructors, it can make your life easier by automatically declaring and defining an implicit default constructor.

In other words, if you write a class type with no default constructor:

```cpp
class Example {
public:
    const std::string& name() const { return name_; }
private:
    std::string name_;
};
```

Then the compiler will create an implicit empty constructor:

```cpp
inline Example() noexcept { }
```

A simple rule is that if a class has no user-declared constructors, the compiler will create a default one if possible.

Have a look:

Ex 2.8. Implicit default constructor. Run @Compiler Explorer

```cpp
struct Value {
    int x;
};

struct CtorValue {
    CtorValue(int v): x{v} { }
    int x;
};

int main() {
    Value v;            // fine, default constructor available
    // CtorValue y;     // error! no default ctor available
    CtorValue z{10};    // using custom ctor
}
```

As you can see above, the compiler will create an implicit default constructor for the `Value` class (since it has no other constructors), but it won't generate a default constructor for the `CtorValue` class. Also, notice that `Value::x` will have an indeterminate value as a default constructor is empty and won't set any value for x.

 Default constructors only default-initialize data members, so in the case of built-in types, it means indeterminate values!

You can control the creation of such a default constructor using two keywords, `default` and `delete`. In short, `default` tells the compiler to use the default implementation, while `delete` blocks the implementation.

Ex 2.9. Default and Delete Constructors. Run @Compiler Explorer

```cpp
struct Value {
    Value() = default;
    int x;
};

struct CtorValue {
    CtorValue() = default;
    CtorValue(int v): x{v} { }
    int x;
};

struct DeletedValue {
    DeletedValue() = delete;
    DeletedValue(int v): x{v} { }
    int x;
};

int main() {
    Value v;           // fine, default constructor available
    CtorValue y;       // ok now, default ctor available
    CtorValue z{10};   // using custom ctor
    // DeletedValue w;    // err, deleted ctor!
    DeletedValue u{10}; // using custom ctor
}
```

In the above example, you can see that we declare `Value() = default;` this tells the compiler to create an empty (doing nothing) implementation. Also, in the `CtorValue` class, we also use the same technique, and, as you can notice, the default construction works now. The third class has `= delete` as its default constructor, and you'll get an error if you want to create an object of this class using its default constructor.

The implicit default constructor will only be created if your type has default-constructible data members or inherits from a default-constructible type. That includes references, `const` data members, unions, and others. See the complete list here @C++Reference[17].

 You may also ask what's the difference between `Value() = default` and `Value() { };` they are both "empty". Still, according to the C++ Standard, the first constructor is *user-declared*, but *not user-provided*, while the second constructor is considered *user-declared* and *user-provided*[18]. We'll cover that later once we cover copy constructors in the section: Trivial classes and user-declared/user-provided default constructors.

Explicit constructors and conversions

Before we move on, it's essential to tackle one important case: the `explicit` keyword, which can be applied before a constructor declaration.

Why is it important? And what does this keyword mean?

In short, it prevents implicit conversions and makes code easier to read.

As an experiment, let's start with the following code:

```cpp
struct Product {
    Product() : name{"default product"}, value{} { }
    Product(int v) : name{"basic"}, value{v} { }
    Product(const std::string& n, int v)
        : name{n}, value{v} { }

    std::string name;
    int value;
};
```

The code looks fine, but now you can create `Product` objects in a bit unusual way:

```cpp
Product numbers = 100.2;         // copy initialization
Product box = {"a box", 1};      // copy list-initialization
```

---

[17]https://en.cppreference.com/w/cpp/language/default_constructor#Deleted_implicitly-declared_default_constructor
[18]Thanks to Timur Doumler for sorting that out.

We can read that those two lines create products, but what values do the data members get? It needs to be clarified! The case in the first line is especially interesting, as I passed a double value of `100.2`, and the compiler tried to convert it into the `int` type (a narrowing conversion) and then passed it to the constructor.

What's more, it's even more problematic with implicit conversions for function calls:

Ex 2.10. Implicit Conversions. Run @Compiler Explorer

```cpp
void printProduct(const Product& prod) {
    std::cout << prod.name << ", " << prod.value << '\n';
}

int main() {
    double someRandomNumber = 100.1;
    printProduct(someRandomNumber);
    printProduct({"a box", 2});
}
```

The output:

```
basic, 100
a box, 2
```

The key idea is to understand: when you pass arguments into a function call, then the compiler performs copy initialization on the arguments.

As you can see, the main issue is with constructors that take only one argument (or have other arguments set to some default value). But even with several arguments, the conversion can happen when you pass an initialization list.

To prevent such unwanted and unexpected conversions, it's good to apply the `explicit` keyword.

When we apply it:

```cpp
explicit Product(int v) : name{"basic"}, value{v} { }
explicit Product(const std::string& n, int v) : name{n}, value{v} { }
```

The compiler will report the following errors:

```
In function 'int main()':
error: invalid initialization of reference of type 'const Product&'
from expression of type 'double'
   28 |        printProduct(someRandomNumber);
      |                     ^~~~~~~~~~~~~~~~
error: converting to 'const Product' from initializer list would use
explicit constructor 'Product::Product(const std::string&, int)'
   29 |        printProduct({"a box", 2});
      |                     ~~~~~~~~^~~~~
```

See the complete example @Compiler Explorer[19].

To fix the code, you need to tell the compiler to create a type explicitly:

```
int someRandomNumber = 100;
printProduct(Product{someRandomNumber});
```

From a practical point of view, the case with a multi-parameter constructor and initializer list is not an issue. The compiler will call the proper constructor and won't perform any narrowing conversions. That's why usually, there's no sense in marking multi-parameter constructors with `explicit`. For example:

```
Product toy = {"a toy", 1.5};
printProduct({"a box", 2.0});
```

The code generates errors about `narrowing conversion ... from double to int`. See the code @Compiler Explorer[20].

Constructors not declared with the `explicit` keyword, also called *converting constructors*. They take part in the implicit conversion sequence. In C++03, those constructors must also be callable with a single argument, but that limitation was lifted in C++11. More on the implicit conversion in a separate section in this chapter.

---

[19]https://godbolt.org/z/3KT5MfnT8
[20]https://godbolt.org/z/7Kab4eT5T

Difference between direct and copy initialization

After addressing several examples of explicit constructors, we can finally answer the differences between direct vs. copy initialization.

We have two primary ways for initialization. Copy:

```cpp
int x = 42;         // a form of a copy initialization

void foo(int param) { }
foo(x);             // copy initialization is performed on the argument

int func() { return 42; }  // a copy initialization done on the return value
struct Point { int x; int y; };
Point pt { 0, 1 };              // aggregate initialization
Point p2 = { 10, 11 };          // uses copy initialization for each element
```

And here's the basic syntax for the direct initialization:

```cpp
int y {42};        // a form of a direct initialization
double z (42.2);   // direct with parens
```

In summary:

- Direct initialization behaves like a function call to an overloaded function: The functions, in this case, are the constructors of the type (including explicit ones). Overload resolution will find the best matching constructor and, when needed, will do any implicit conversion required.
- Copy initialization constructs an implicit conversion sequence: It tries to convert arguments to an object of the given type. Explicit constructors are not considered for copy initialization.

For example, since aggregate initialization uses copy initialization to init subobjects, this code won't work:

```cpp
struct Point {
    explicit Point(int a, int b): x{a}, y{b} { }
    int x;
    int y;
};

struct Aggregate {
    int a;
    Point p;
};

int main() {
    Aggregate ag { 0, {0, 1}};     // <<
    Aggregate ag2 = { 0, {0, 1}}; // <<
}
```

GCC reports the following error:

```
error: converting to 'Point' from initializer list would use explicit construct\
or 'Point::Point(int, int)'
   19 |    Aggregate ag { 0, {0, 1}};
```

To fix this, you need to mention the type name explicitly:

```cpp
int main() {
    Aggregate ag { 0, Point{0, 1}};
    Aggregate ag2 = { 0, Point{0, 1}};
}
```

See the working code @Compiler Explorer[21].

Even more

The `explicit` keyword is so important that it has its own rule in C++ Core Guidelines: C++ Core Guidelines - C.46[22].

---

[21]https://godbolt.org/z/d8cronMM1
[22]https://isocpp.github.io/CppCoreGuidelines/CppCoreGuidelines#Rc-explicit

> C.46. By default, declare single-argument constructors `explicit`
>
> **Reason**: To avoid unintended conversions.

 Additionally, in C++20, we have an extended syntax `explicit(bool)` to mark explicit constructors conditionally. This is a bit advanced feature, so we won't address this in this book. You can read more @C++Reference[23].

Implicit conversion and converting constructors

While it's best to use `explicit` constructors, there are some cases where implicit conversion saves the day. Let's have a look at several constructors from the Standard Library:

```
// optional:
template <class U> constexpr optional(U&& value);

// std::string:
constexpr basic_string(const CharT* s, size_type count, /*allocator*/);

// pair
template<class U1 = T1, class U2 = T2> constexpr pair(U1&& x, U2&& y);
```

As you can see, for "wrapper" types, it's usually handy to initialize them from the "wrapped" type. For example:

```
void foo(const std::string& s) { }
foo("Hello World");
std::optional<int> optX = 10;
std::pair<int, double> p = { 10, 10.5};
```

Above, all of the expression uses copy initialization, and thus explicit constructors wouldn't be used. It's very convenient to pass `"Hello World"` which is `const char*` rather than calling:

---
[23]https://en.cppreference.com/w/cpp/language/explicit

```
foo(std::string{"Hello World"});
```

 When designed carefully, types that wrap other types are suitable to have converting constructors. In C++20, it's even possible to set a conditional `explicit` constructor when the wrapped type has `explicit` constructors. Read more in C++20's Conditionally Explicit Constructors - C++ Team Blog[24].

It's also good to know that the compiler is not allowed to chain multiple conversion sequences. For example:

```
struct Number {
    Number(int n) { }
};
struct Special {
    Special(Number num) {}
};
```

In the above case, you can call:

```
Special spec { 42 };
```

This will use a single conversion sequence from 42 (an `int`) to `Number`, and then it will call the `Special(Number num)` constructor.

On the other hand, the copy syntax won't work:

```
Special spec = 42; // doesn't compile!
```

This one doesn't compile because the compiler would have to first convert the integer into `Number` and then `Number` into `Special`.

Based on C++ Reference - copy initialization[25]:

---

[24]https://devblogs.microsoft.com/cppblog/c20s-conditionally-explicit-constructors/
[25]https://en.cppreference.com/w/cpp/language/copy_initialization

> For T object = other;: If T is a class type, and the cv-unqualified version of the type of other is not T or derived from T, or if T is non-class type, but the type of other is a class type, user-defined conversion sequences that can convert from the type of other to T (or to a type derived from T if T is a class type and a conversion function is available) are examined and the best one is selected through overload resolution. The result of the conversion, which is a prvalue expression of the cv-unqualified version of T if a converting constructor was used, is then used to direct-initialize the object.

The key rule here is that the compiler can perform only **one** conversion step, and our example requires two steps. That's why we'll get an error (see @Compiler Explorer[26]). You can fix the code by making conversion explicit:

```
Number n = 42;
Special spec = n;
```

We can find the full rule in the C++ Standard over.ics.user[27]:

> A user-defined conversion sequence consists of an initial standard conversion sequence followed by a user-defined conversion followed by a second standard conversion sequence.

Read more in Standard conversions[28] and User-Defined Type Conversions[29] @Microsoft Learn.

Constructor summary

This chapter was one of the longest, as we had to prepare the background for the rest of the book. Once we know the basics of how data members can be initialized through constructors, we can move further and explore various new C++ features and examples. Now, it's time to investigate two other types of constructors: copy and move. Read on to the next chapter.

---

[26]https://godbolt.org/z/dscvKG65f
[27]https://timsong-cpp.github.io/cppwp/n4868/over.ics.user#def:conversion_sequence,user-defined
[28]https://learn.microsoft.com/en-us/cpp/cpp/standard-conversions?view=msvc-170
[29]https://learn.microsoft.com/en-us/cpp/cpp/user-defined-type-conversions-cpp?view=msvc-170

3. Copy and Move Operations

Regular constructors allow you to invoke some logic and initialize data members when an object is created from a list of arguments. But C++ also has two special constructor types that let you control a situation when an object is created using an instance of the same class type. Those constructors are called copy and move constructors. Additionally, you can provide custom assignment operators that the compiler calls when you assign new values to existing objects. Let's have a look.

Copy constructor

A copy constructor is a special member function taking an object of the same type as the first argument, usually by a `const` reference.

```
ClassName(const ClassName&);
```

Technically it might have other parameters, but they all have to have default values assigned, and in practice, it's very uncommon. The compiler calls a copy constructor when you initialize an object using a variable of the same type (through copy initialization or direct initialization), and there's no better match (like a move constructor or a regular constructor). Below you can find a few examples of a call to a copy constructor:

```
Product base { 42, "base product" }; // an initial object
Product other { base };    // direct list initialization
Product another(base);     // direct initialization with parens
Product oneMore = base;    // copy initialization
std::array<Product, 3> arr = { base, other, oneMore }; // each elem
Product foo(Product p) {
    Product temp{"from foo", p.id};
    return temp; // copy initialization
}
Product x;
foo(x); // copy initialization, copy into an argument
```

We'll discuss all of the above forms in the further section.

As a mental model, we can assume that most classes have their default, compiler-generated copy constructor. Such a default copy constructor performs a memberwise copy of each data member. In short, the compiler visits each member and calls the member's copy constructor (with some potential optimizations for trivial, built-in data types). Thanks to this approach, you can initialize objects, pass them as arguments or return from functions without any custom implementation in a given type.

However, implementing a copy constructor might be necessary when your class has data members that requires some special attention when copying. Those cases especially include resource handles (files, pointers to memory blocks, etc.). For example, suppose a class contains a pointer to a memory block. When a default copy constructor copies such a pointer, the resulting pointer copy will point to the exact memory location. Similarly, if your class uses a handle to a file, then after the memberwise copy, the handle will be copied, and two objects will relate to the same file. Depending on the program requirements, this might not be what you want. In a case with pointers, it's usually better to allocate a new memory block and copy the data of that block.

The situation for a shallow copy is illustrated by the following diagram:

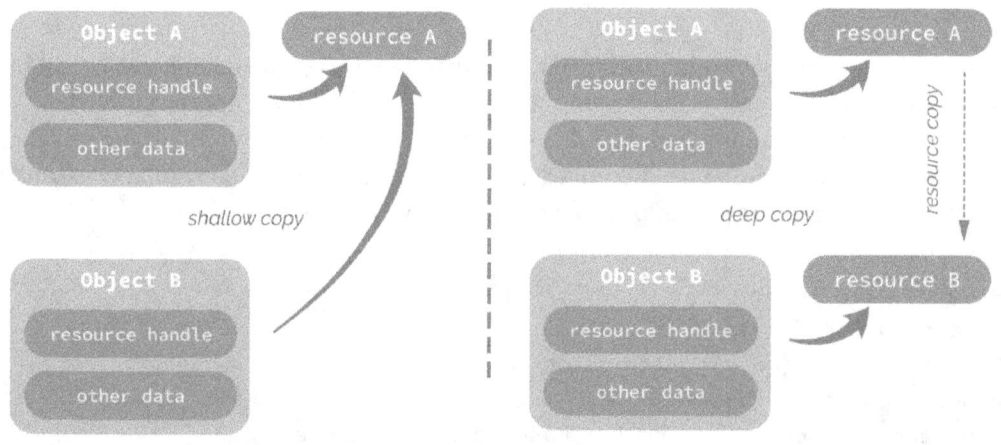

Shallow vs. Deep Copy

On the diagram, you can see a comparison of a shallow (bitwise copy) vs. the deep copy approach. If you copy the resource handles, the resulting object will point to the same resource. For the full version, you need to copy the resource and then correctly assign the resource handle to that new copy.

Standard library containers like std::vector or std::string internally contain pointers to memory buffers to store the elements. They all have explicitly defined copy constructors that support full data copy, so when you copy one vector to another, the memory buffers will also be copied. You don't have to think about those internal mechanisms when using those types in your code.

A canonical implementation of a copy constructor

Implementing a copy constructor is straightforward and very similar to regular constructors. The only difference is that you have a single parameter which is a (const) reference to an object of that same type.

For the Product class, we can write the following:

```
class Product {
public:
    explicit Product(int id, const std::string& name)
        : id_{id}, name_{name} {
        std::cout << "Product(): " << id_ << ", " << name_ << '\n';
    }
    // copy constructor
    Product(const Product& other)
        : id_{other.id_}, name_{other.name_} { }
private:
    int id_;
    std::string name_;
};
```

As you can see, the copy constructor uses the member initialization list to copy the data from other. Please notice that there's no need to use public getters, as we have access to all private data members. The syntax requires a reference, so writing Product(Product other) won't be treated as a copy constructor (otherwise, it could lead to recursive calls).

A copy constructor can also take a non-const argument like Product(Product& other). However, such a constructor might modify the other object and make code harder to read and understand. It might be better to use move semantics and move constructors when you want to "steal" the guts of some other object.

Copy constructors can be marked with `explicit`, but this is not a common practice and might prevent copy initialization.

Here's another example where basic logging is enabled. Such console output is helpful to see when constructors are called:

Ex 3.1. Logging in a copy constructor. Run @Compiler Explorer

```cpp
class Product {
public:
    explicit Product(int id, const std::string& name)
        : id_{id}, name_{name} {
        std::cout << "Product(): " << id_ << ", " << name_ << '\n';
    }
    Product(const Product& other)
        : id_{other.id_}, name_{other.name_} {
        std::cout << "Product(copy): " << id_ << ", " << name_ << '\n';
    }
    const std::string& name() const { return name_; }
private:
    int id_;
    std::string name_;
};
```

And here's the code that creates `Product` objects:

Ex 3.1. Logging in a copy constructor, demo. Run @Compiler Explorer

```cpp
void foo(Product p) { std::cout << "inside foo()\n"; }
int main() {
    Product base { 42, "base product" }; // an initial object
    std::cout << base.Name() << " created\n";
    std::cout << "Product other { base };\n";
    Product other { base };
    std::cout << "Product another(base);\n";
    Product another(base);
    std::cout << "Product oneMore = base;\n";
    Product oneMore = base;
    std::cout << "std::array<Product, 2> = { base, other };\n";
```

```
        std::array<Product, 2> arr = { base, other };
        std::cout << "calling foo()\n";
        foo(arr[0]);
}
```

If you run the code, you should see the following output:

```
Product(): 42, base product
base product created
Product other { base };
Product(copy): 42, base product
Product another(base);
Product(copy): 42, base product
Product oneMore = base;
Product(copy): 42, base product
std::array<Product, 2> = { base, other };
Product(copy): 42, base product
Product(copy): 42, base product
calling foo()
Product(copy): 42, base product
inside foo()
```

At the start of the `main()` function, we construct base product, and then use it to copy-construct all other instances: other, another, and oneMore. Each time a copy constructor is called. The same happens for `std::array<Product, 2>`. Later we call a function `foo()`, and when you pass an argument as a value, a copy has to be created using a copy constructor call.

Copy elision

Now, let's consider the following code:

```cpp
Product createProduct() {
    Product temp{101, "from createProduct()"};
    return temp;
}

int main() {
    std::cout << "calling createProduct()\n";
    Product created = createProduct();
}
```

The output is:

```
calling createProduct()
Product(): 101, from createProduct()
```

This result contradicts what I wrote before: a copy constructor should be called for return statements. Technically, it should, but the output shows a regular constructor only.

This feature is a compiler optimization that allows it to "elide" such extra object copies. To be precise, it's called Named Return Value Optimization (NRVO[1]), as there's a named variable that we "reuse". The compiler can see through the initialization, deduce that the `temp` object is used only to initialize `created`, and can "compress" the creation steps. The GCC compiler has a switch to turn off such optimization: `-fno-elide-constructors`.

If you compile with that flag, you should be able to see the following:

```
calling createProduct()
Product(): 101, from createProduct()
Product(copy): 101, from createProduct()
```

Have a look @Compiler Explorer[2].

But there's more!

---
[1] https://en.cppreference.com/w/cpp/language/copy_elision
[2] https://godbolt.org/z/49M1GaxK6

Starting from C++17, there's a mandatory copy elision, also called "deferred temporary materialization". While the previous example was an optional compiler optimization, we have language rules that clearly express the new behavior this time. Not going into details, it will elide additional copies when there's an unnamed temporary object from which we initialize a new entity: For example:

Ex 3.3. Copy elision, C++17. Run @Compiler Explorer

```
Product createProduct() {
    return {101, "from createProduct()"};
}

int main() {
    std::cout << "calling createProduct()\n";
    Product created = createProduct();
}
```

This time the compiler will always generate the following output:

```
calling createProduct()
Product(): 101, from createProduct()
```

In other words, the temporary from `createProduct` is skipped and used to initialize the `created` object directly. This feature is helpful for optimization and efficiently working with non-copyable and non-movable types types that previously couldn't be returned from factory functions.

If you want to know more about this feature, have a look at my book: C++17 in Detail[3] or see this blog post:Guaranteed Copy Elision Does Not Elide Copies[4] @VisualC++ Team Blog.

A compiler-generated copy constructor

The compiler will generate an implicit copy constructor for you if your class complies with the following key rules:

- All non-static data members that can be copied (their copy constructors are accessible, not `delete`),

---

[3] https://leanpub.com/cpp17indetail
[4] https://devblogs.microsoft.com/cppblog/guaranteed-copy-elision-does-not-elide-copies/

- Your class has no base classes, or a direct or virtual base class that can be copied,
- Your class doesn't have any data members of rvalue reference type,
- Your class doesn't have a user-defined copy assignment operator and a user-defined destructor,
- Your class doesn't have a user-defined move constructor or move assignment operator,

You can find all the rules in this handy list @C++Reference[5].

As an example, let's have a look at the following code:

Ex 3.4. A non-default copy constructor. Run @Compiler Explorer

```cpp
#include <iostream>
#include <string>

struct Name {
    explicit Name(const std::string& str): name_{str} { }
    Name(const Name&) = delete;
    std::string name_;
};

class Product {
public:
    explicit Product(int id, const std::string& name)
        : id_{id}, name_{name} {
        std::cout << "Product(): " << id_ << ", " << name_.name_ << '\n';
    }
private:
    int id_;
    Name name_;
};

int main() {
    Product first{10, "basic"};
    Product second { first };
}
```

Please look at the line where we are trying to call the copy constructor. It won't compile:

[5]https://en.cppreference.com/w/cpp/language/copy_constructor#Deleted_implicitly-declared_copy_constructor

```
<source>:10:7: note: 'Product::Product(const Product&)' is implicitly
deleted because the default definition would be ill-formed:
   10 |  class Product {
      |        ^~~~~~~
```

The compiler tells us it cannot create a copy constructor because the `name` data member cannot be copied, as it has deleted the copy constructor.

We can also observe this by looking at the output from C++Insights @see this link[6]:

```
public:
// inline Product(const Product &) = delete;
// inline Product(Product &&) = delete;
// inline ~Product() noexcept = default;
```

Move constructor

Move constructors take rvalue references of the same type. Usually, such a constructor has the following form:

```
ClassName(ClassName&&) noexcept;
```

Let's try to decipher the full syntax.

In short, rvalue references are temporary objects, usually appearing on the right-hand side of an expression, and whose value is about to expire.

For example:

```
std::string hello { "Hello Amazing"};    // lvalue, a regular object
std::string world { " Programming World"}; // lvalue
std::string msg = hello + world;
```

Above, the expression `hello + world` creates a temporary object. It doesn't have a name, and we cannot access it easily. Such temporary objects will end their lifetime immediately

---

[6]https://cppinsights.io/s/15ea2cb1

after the expression completes (unless it's assigned to a `const` or rvalue reference[7]), so we can steal resources from them safely. It doesn't make sense in the case of built-in types like integers or floats, as we need to copy values anyway. But in the case of strings or memory buffers, we can avoid data copy and reassign the pointers. The situation is illustrated with the following diagram:

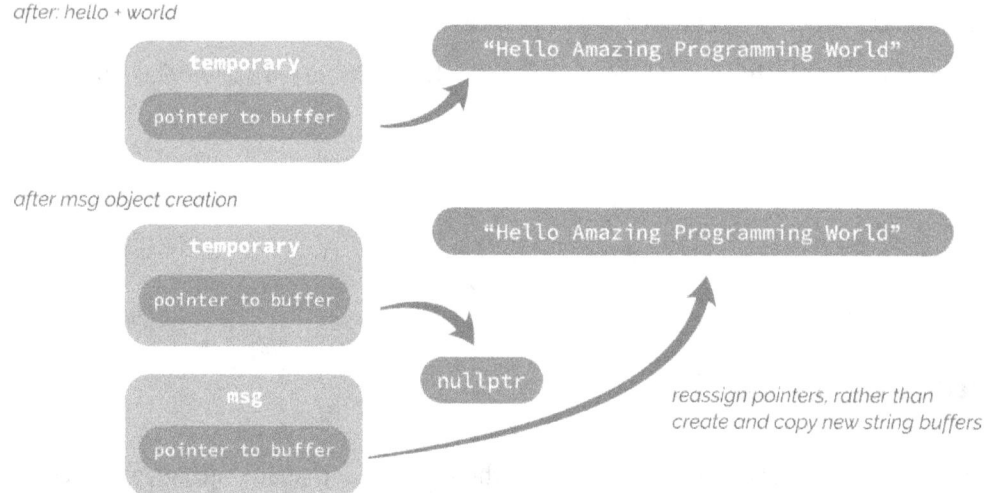

Idea of a move constructor

The diagram illustrates the state after computing `hello + world` and later when `msg` is initialized. The compiler creates a temporary object with a long string, stored in a buffer allocated outside the string. The string object has a pointer to that buffer. Later, `msg` is created from that temporary object. We know that the object will expire so that we can reassign the pointers to the memory buffers. `msg` gets a pointer to the long string. The temporary object gets `nullptr` (conceptually, as the internal implementation might differ).

Move constructors are a way to support the case with initialization from temporary objects. In many cases, they are an optimization over regular copy constructor calls. Additionally, they can also be used to pass "ownership" of the resource, for example, with smart pointers.

You can mark a regular object as expiring with the `std::move` function when you have a regular object with a name. This tells the compiler that the object's value is no longer needed, so it's safe to "steal" resources from it.

Have a look at this example:

---

[7] The lifetime of a temporary object may be extended by binding to a const lvalue reference or to an rvalue reference. See more at https://en.cppreference.com/w/cpp/language/lifetime.

Ex 3.5. Move constructor. Run @Compiler Explorer

```cpp
#include <iostream>
#include <string>

class Product {
public:
    explicit Product(int id, const std::string& name)
        : id_{id}, name_{name} {
        std::cout << "Product(): " << id_ << ", " << name_ << '\n';
    }
    Product(Product&& other) noexcept
        : id_{other.id_}, name_{std::move(other.name_)} {
        std::cout << "Product(move): " << id_ << ", " << name_ << '\n';
    }
    const std::string& name() const { return name_; }
private:
    int id_;
    std::string name_;
};

int main() {
    Product tvSet {100, "tv set"};
    std::cout << tvSet.name() << " created...\n";
    Product setV2 { std::move(tvSet) };
    std::cout << setV2.name() << " created...\n";
    std::cout << "old value: " << tvSet.name() << '\n';
}
```

When you run the code, you can see the following output:

```
Product(): 100, tv set
tv set created...
Product(move): 100, tv set
tv set created...
old value:
```

As you can see, we create the first object, and then mark it as expiring. This gives a chance for the compiler to call the move constructor.

```
Product(Product&& other) noexcept
    : id_(other.id_), name_(std::move(other.name_))
```

The above implementation is similar to a copy constructor, but we must pay attention to details. Since `id_` is just an integer, all we can do is copy the value. We cannot perform any optimizations here. For the `name_` member, we can initialize it with `std::move(other.name_)`. We encounter the first problem, `other.name_` is a name, so not temporary (a temporary has no name); we can not move (take, steal) its contents. That is why we tell the compiler to interpret it as temporary by using the expression `std::move(other.name_)`. This will invoke the move constructor for `std::string`, and, potentially, "steal" the buffer from `other.name_`.

The move constructor must ensure that the other object is left in an unspecified but valid state (so that it can be still deleted or assigned with a new value). In our case, we can see it in the last line of the output. The line `old value:` ends with nothing, so the string was cleared.

 Move constructors can be marked with `explicit`, but it's not a common practice and might affect generic code that relies on implicit move constructors (like standard algorithms).

`noexcept` and move constructors

While I mentioned that `noexcept` wouldn't be covered in this book, I need to make one exception to this rule. The fundamental principle for `noexcept` on a function declaration is to guarantee that the function won't return any exceptions (won't throw from the function scope). If it does, the compiler must call `std::terminate()` instead of regular exception handling. Having a `noexcept` function allows the compiler and the libraries to optimize the code.

For example, when you have a `std::vector` of `T`, if `T` has move operations marked with `noexcept`, the vector is allowed to perform resize operations with move rather than copy (to guarantee safety). To illustrate this behavior, I modified the `Product` class and added a copy constructor:

```cpp
Product(const Product& other) : id_{other.id_}, name_{other.name_} {
    std::cout << "Product(copy): " << id_ << ", " << name_ << '\n';
}
Product(Product&& other) : id_{other.id_}, name_{std::move(other.name_)} {
    std::cout << "Product(move): " << id_ << ", " << name_ << '\n';
}
```

Notice that there's no `noexcept` in the move constructor. Now, if we run the following demo code:

Ex 3.6. Copy on resize for `std::vector`. Run @Compiler Explorer

```cpp
int main() {
    std::vector<Product> prods;
    prods.emplace_back(101, "car");
    prods.emplace_back(202, "box");
    prods.emplace_back(303, "toy");
    prods.emplace_back(404, "mug");
    prods.emplace_back(505, "pencil");
}
```

We'll see the following output:

```
Product(): 101, car
Product(): 202, box
Product(copy): 101, car
Product(): 303, toy
Product(copy): 101, car
Product(copy): 202, box
Product(): 404, mug
Product(): 505, pencil
Product(copy): 101, car
Product(copy): 202, box
Product(copy): 303, toy
Product(copy): 404, mug
```

Let's try to decipher the output.

The `emplace_back` function (available since C++11) creates a new element at the end of the container using the arguments you pass. Alternatively, we could use `push_back`, but this requires an additional copy (or move) of the Product object. When we add the first element, you can see that a regular constructor is called. Now, with the second element, the vector must grow its internal buffer and copy existing elements to a new buffer. That's why you can see a regular constructor for the "box" object and then a copy constructor for "car". Similarly, when I add the third element, its constructor is called, and then copies of "car" and "box" must be invoked. Later the process continues as we add more elements and the container grows. It's implementation-specific, but usually, std::vector might grow 1.5x or 2x each time it has to resize. For example, it starts with one element and a capacity of one, then two elements and a capacity of 2, 3 elements and a capacity of 4, 5 elements and a capacity of 6 or 8, and so on. This helps to amortize the cost of adding new values.

Now, let's modify the move constructor and make it noexcept:

Ex 3.7. Move on resize for std::vector. Run @Compiler Explorer

```
Product(Product&& other) noexcept
    : id_{other.id_}, name_{std::move(other.name_)} {
    std::cout << "Product(move): " << id_ << ", " << name_ << '\n';
}
```

When we run the code, you'll see the following log:

```
Product(): 101, car
Product(): 202, box
Product(move): 101, car
Product(): 303, toy
Product(move): 101, car
Product(move): 202, box
Product(): 404, mug
Product(): 505, pencil
Product(move): 101, car
Product(move): 202, box
Product(move): 303, toy
Product(move): 404, mug
```

Now, the compiler calls a move constructor rather than a copy! In many cases, this can be much faster than copying data, as we can copy pointers rather than copying the entire content of a string. It's implementation-depended if the library uses that optimization technique, but MSVC, GCC, and Clang library implementations stick to this rule.

Below you can find a basic illustration of this "growth" process:

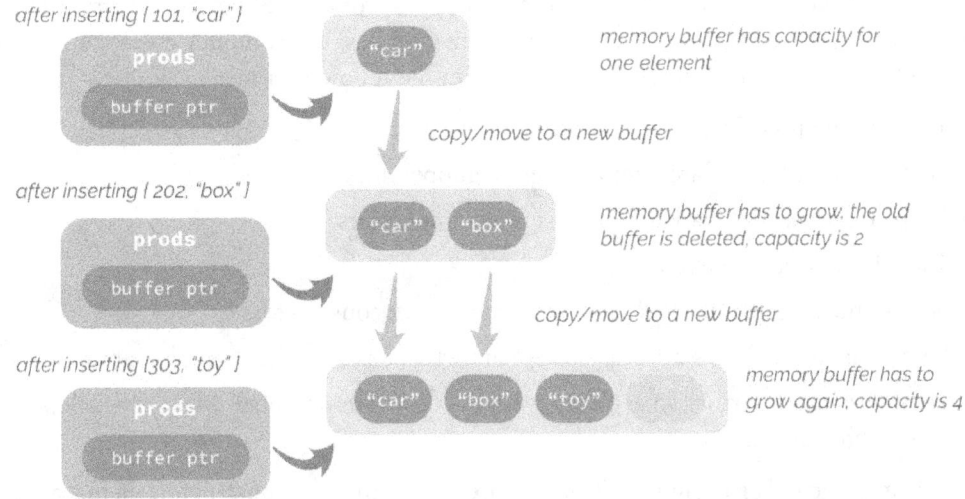

Vector resize process for three elements

On the diagram, on the left-hand side, you can see the prods vector that has a pointer to a memory buffer with all elements. The vector class usually contains other data members, like size and capacity, but we'll stick to the simple model. After inserting the first element, the buffer has a capacity for only one object and then has to grow if we add more values. In the third line, you can see a new buffer with three elements but a "transparent" spot for a fourth one. Each time a buffer is recreated, it must copy/move existing elements.

The reason for this technique is that when the move constructor is not marked with noexcept then the container has to be prepared for a case where it tries to copy elements to a new buffer, and at some point, one operation throws. The only way to revert to a safe situation is to abandon the copy[8] and leave the container in the previous state. When move noexcept is available, then the vector implementation can assume that there's no exception happening, and moving will be "safe" for all elements. Other algorithms from the Standard Library, like std::sort, might also benefit from having noexcept guarantees on move operations.

You can read more about this approach in the following C++ Core Guideline: C.66: Make move operations noexcept[9]. And also in this detailed article by Andrzej Krzemieński: Using noexcept @Andrzej's C++ blog[10].

---

[8]C++ defines exception safety guarantees like strong, basic, none. See more at https://en.cppreference.com/w/cpp/language/exceptions#Exception_safety
[9]https://isocpp.github.io/CppCoreGuidelines/CppCoreGuidelines#c66-make-move-operations-noexcept
[10]https://akrzemi1.wordpress.com/2011/06/10/using-noexcept/

A compiler-generated move constructor

Don't worry! If your class uses built-in types or types from the Standard Library, there's no need to write custom move constructors. In most cases, the compiler creates a default implementation assuming your class complies with the following rules:

- There are no user-declared copy constructors.
- There are no user-declared copy assignment operators.
- There are no user-declared move assignment operators.
- There is no user-declared destructor.
- Non-static data members all have accessible move constructors.
- Your class has no bases classes, a direct or virtual base class that can be moved.
- Your class has a virtual base class or a non-static data member without a deleted or inaccessible destructor.

The rules are logical. For example, if you declare a custom copy constructor, there's a high chance your class require some special attention, and thus move operations should also be implemented by you rather than the compiler. Additionally, if you have a copy constructor but no move constructor, the compiler will call the copy.

You can find all the rules in this handy list @C++Reference[11].

Distinguishing from assignment

It's crucial to distinguish cases where the compiler invokes a copy or move constructor from cases where it invokes the assignment operator. The code might look similar, but it behaves differently.

C++ gives us the powerful capability to implement operators for user-defined types. Such operators make it easier and more natural for operations related to math, string manipulation, relations, and stream output or input, among others. For example, `std::string` implements `operator+` for string concatenation. Similarly, you can define `operator-` for classes representing 3D Vectors in space. You can see the complete list of operators on operator overloading @C++Reference[12].

If you don't provide a custom declaration, then the compiler attempts to define an implicit version. While most operators won't work for user-defined types and don't exist until you

---

[11] https://en.cppreference.com/w/cpp/language/move_constructor#Implicitly-declared_move_constructor
[12] https://en.cppreference.com/w/cpp/language/operators

implement them, there's a special `operator=`, called the assignment operator. By default, the implicit version calls the assignment operator for sub-objects of the given type. For example:

```cpp
struct Point { int x; int y; };

Point pt { 10, 10 };
Point another { 100, 100 };
another = pt;              // implicit assignment operator called!
```

Even though I don't provide any implementation for `operator=`, the compiler defines it, and I can write the assignment: `another = pt`. By default, the operator copies data members from `pt` into `another`. Since the `Point` type is trivial and uses built-in types for its data members, we'll get a bitwise copy of `pt`.

In a basic form, we can implement the assignment operator in at least two forms:

```cpp
// copy assignment operator
Product& operator=(const Product& other) { /* ... */ }
```

Or

```cpp
// move assignment operator
Product& operator=(Product&& other) { /* ... */ }
```

The copy assignment operator will be called when there's an lvalue on the right-hand side of the assignment expression. The move assignment is called when there's an rvalue reference.

See the following code, where I implemented a copy assignment for the `Product` class:

Ex 3.8. Copy assignment for Product. Run @Compiler Explorer

```cpp
class Product {
public:
    explicit Product(int id, const std::string& name)
        : id_{id}, name_{name} {
        std::cout << "Product(): " << id_ << ", " << name_ << '\n';
    }
    Product(const Product& other) : id_{other.id_}, name_{other.name_} {
        std::cout << "Product(copy): " << id_ << ", " << name_ << '\n';
    }
```

```cpp
    Product& operator=(const Product& other) {
        if (this == &other)
            return *this;

        id_ = other.id_;
        name_ = other.name_;
        std::cout << "operator=(copy): " << id_ << ", " << name_ << '\n';
        return *this;
    }
    const std::string& name() const { return name_; }
private:
    int id_;
    std::string name_;
};
```

And here's the demo code:

```cpp
Product base { 42, "base" };
Product first { base };     // copy ctor called!
Product second = first;     // copy ctor called!
Product third { 100, "third" };
third = second; // assignment operator called!
```

The compiler calls a copy constructor when you initialize an object. When an entity already exists, the program runs an assignment operation.

And here's the corresponding version of the move assignment operator:

Ex 3.9. Move assignment for Product. Run @Compiler Explorer

```cpp
class Product {
public:
    explicit Product(int id, const std::string& name)
        : id_{id}, name_{name} {
        std::cout << "Product(): " << id_ << ", " << name_ << '\n';
    }
    Product(Product&& other) noexcept
        : id_{other.id_}, name_{std::move(other.name_)} {
        std::cout << "Product(move): " << id_ << ", " << name_ << '\n';
```

```cpp
    }
    Product& operator=(Product&& other) noexcept {
        id_ = other.id_;
        name_ = std::move(other.name_);
        std::cout << "operator=(move): " << id_ << ", " << name_ << '\n';
        return *this;
    }
    const std::string& name() const { return name_; }
private:
    int id_;
    std::string name_;
};
```

```cpp
Product base { 42, "base" };
Product first { std::move(base) };  // move ctor called!
std::cout << "base.name() after move: " << base.name() << '\n';
Product second = std::move(first);  // move ctor called!
std::cout << "first.name() after move: " << first.name() << '\n';
Product third { 100, "third" };
third = std::move(second); // assignment operator called!
std::cout << "second.name() after move: " << second.name() << '\n';
```

Above, we can explicitly ask to call a move constructor when we use `std::move` and mark an object as expiring. When an object exists and we assign a new value, the assignment operator will be called. If we run the code above, you'll get the following output:

```
Product(): 42, base
Product(move): 42, base
base.name() after move:
Product(move): 42, base
first.name() after move:
Product(): 100, third
operator=(move): 42, base
second.name() after move:
```

As you can see, after we move from an object, it's left in an unspecified but valid state. For strings, it means an empty string.

Adding debug logging to constructors

As an exercise, let's add logging to our `DataPacket` class and see when each constructor is called.

Ex 3.10. Logging in the `DataPacket` class. Run @Compiler Explorer

```cpp
class DataPacket {
    std::string data_;
    size_t checkSum_;
    size_t serverId_;

public:
    DataPacket() : data_{}, checkSum_{0}, serverId_{0} { }

    explicit DataPacket(const std::string& data, size_t serverId)
    : data_{data}, checkSum_{calcCheckSum(data)}, serverId_{serverId} {
        std::cout << "Ctor for \"" << data_ << "\"\n";
    }
    DataPacket(const DataPacket& other)
    : data_{other.data_}
    , checkSum_{other.checkSum_}
    , serverId_{other.serverId_} {
        std::cout << "Copy ctor for \"" << data_ << "\"\n";
    }
    DataPacket(DataPacket&& other) noexcept
    : data_{std::move(other.data_)}   // move string member...
    , checkSum_{other.checkSum_}      // no need to move built-in types...
    , serverId_{other.serverId_} {
        other.checkSum_ = 0; // leave this in a proper state
        std::cout << "Move ctor for \"" << data_ << "\"\n";
    }
    DataPacket& operator=(const DataPacket& other) {
        if (this != &other) {
            data_ = other.data_;
            checkSum_ = other.checkSum_;
            serverId_ = other.serverId_;
            std::cout << "Assignment for \"" << data_ << "\"\n";
        }
```

```cpp
        return *this;
    }
    DataPacket& operator=(DataPacket&& other) noexcept {
        if (this != &other) {
            data_ = std::move(other.data_);
            checkSum_ = other.checkSum_;
            other.checkSum_ = 0; // leave this in a proper state
            serverId_ = other.serverId_;
            std::cout << "Move Assignment for \"" << data_ << "\"\n";
        }
        return *this;
    }
    // getters/setters
};
```

And here's the `main()` function:

Ex 3.10. Logging in the `DataPacket` class, the main function. Run @Compiler Explorer

```cpp
int main() {
    DataPacket firstMsg {"first msg", 101 };
    DataPacket copyMsg { firstMsg };                    // line 3
    DataPacket secondMsg { "second msg", 202 };
    copyMsg = secondMsg;                                // line 5
    DataPacket movedMsg { std::move(secondMsg)}; // line 6
    // now we stole the data, so it should be empty...
    std::cout << "secondMsg's data after move ctor): \""
              << secondMsg.getData() << "\", sum: "
              << secondMsg.getCheckSum() << '\n';
    movedMsg = std::move(firstMsg);                     // line 11
    // now we stole the name, so it should be empty...
    std::cout << "firstMsg's data after move ctor): \""
              << firstMsg.getData() << "\", sum: "
              << firstMsg.getCheckSum() << '\n';
}
```

When you run the example, you should see the following output:

```
Ctor for "first msg"
Copy ctor for "first msg"
Ctor for "second msg"
Assignment for "second msg"
Move ctor for "second msg"
secondMsg's data after move ctor): "", sum: 0
Move Assignment for "first msg"
firstMsg's data after move ctor): "", sum: 0
```

The example creates several `DataPacket` objects, and with each creation, you can see that the compiler invokes the appropriate constructor or assignment operator. For instance, in **line 3**, we need a copy constructor call. On the other hand, **line 5** shows an assignment (`copyMsg` already exists). In the last section of `main()`, **lines 6 and 11**, there are calls to `std::move()`, which marks `secondMsg` and `firstMsg` as an rvalue reference, from which the contents could be moved. This means that the object is unimportant later, and we can "steal" from it. In this case, the compiler will call a move constructor or move assignment operator.

Improvements: The logging part in the example is a bit crude, as the class directly calls a global stream object. In some cases, this might complicate unit testing or using the class in general. It would be better to rely on some configurable "tracing/logging" object that could be passed as a parameter to the constructor. We'll tackle that approach in the section about references as static data members. What's more, we can use Copy And Swap idiom to streamline the assignment operator and copy/move implementations. See more in the Techniques chapter.

Trivial classes and user-provided default constructors

We covered the basics of default, copy and move constructors. And now, we can try to answer a question that might appear several times before: what's the difference between `= default`, declaring a special member function empty `{}`, or not declaring anything?

Let's have a look at the example, assuming we have several similar classes `MyTypeX`:

```cpp
struct MyType0 {
    int x;
};
struct MyType1 {
    MyType1() { }
    int x;
};
struct MyType2 {
    MyType2() = default;
    int x;
};
struct MyType3 {
    MyType3();
    int x;
};
MyType3::MyType3() = default;
```

As you can see, there are four ways you can end up with an "empty" constructor and implicit default copy constructors. The core difference is that in `MyType0` and `MyType2`, default constructors are considered **not user-provided**. Such a term has some consequences in the C++ Standard. For example both `MyType0` and `MyType2` are considered *trivial*. In case of `MyType1` and `MyType3` we have user-provided constructors.

First of all: what does "user-provided" mean? From the Standard dcl.fct.def.default#5[13]:

> A function is user-provided if it is user-declared and not explicitly defaulted or deleted on its first declaration.

```cpp
struct X {
    X() = default;              // 1
    X(const X&) { /*...*/ }     // 2
};
```

Above, the first declaration, //1 is not user-provided. It's user-declared (since we declare it), but since we explicitly =default it, it's not considered user-provided. On the other hand, the

---

[13]https://timsong-cpp.github.io/cppwp/n4868/dcl.fct.def.default#5

copy constructor is user-provided since we provide an implementation. The same happens for `MyType0`, where we don't provide any special member function, or for `MyType2`, where we declare a default constructor, but we explicitly make it `default`, and thus it's not user-provided. In the case of `MyType3` on its first declaration we don't default it, we only create an implementation by making it `=default`. So this constructor is still user-provided.

According to the C++ Standard[14]:

> A trivial class is a class that is trivially copyable and has one or more eligible default constructors, all of which are trivial.

And a *trivially copyable* class is:

> A trivially copyable class is a class:
> - that has at least one eligible copy constructor, move constructor, copy assignment operator, or move assignment operator,
> - where each eligible copy constructor, move constructor, copy assignment operator, and move assignment operator is trivial, and
> - that has a trivial, non-deleted destructor.

Now, we have to understand *a trivial special member function*. For default constructors, see this section in the C++ Standard - class.default.ctor#3[15]:

> A default constructor is trivial if it is not user-provided and if:
> - its class has no virtual functions and no virtual base classes, and
> - no non-static data member of its class has a default member initializer, and
> - all the direct base classes of its class have trivial default constructors, and
> - for all the non-static data members of its class that are of class type (or array thereof), each such class has a trivial default constructor.

---

[14]https://timsong-cpp.github.io/cppwp/n4868/class.prop#1
[15]https://timsong-cpp.github.io/cppwp/n4868/class.default.ctor#3

For copy/move constructors, see this section in the C++ Standard - class.copy.ctor#11[16]:

> A copy/move constructor for class X is trivial if it is not user-provided and if:
> - class X has no virtual functions and no virtual base classes, and
> - the constructor selected to copy/move each direct base class subobject is trivial, and
> - for each non-static data member of X that is of class type (or array thereof), the constructor selected to copy/move that member is trivial;

As I mentioned, `MyType0` and `MyType2` are *trivial* because they have trivial default constructors and don't violate any of the above rules. `MyType1` and `MyType3` have empty constructors, but they are *user-provided*, so they cannot be *trivial* types.

We have some definitions, but what are the implications of those slight differences?

- Trivial types occupy a contiguous memory area (including padding).
- They are *"mem-copyable"*, so you can only `memcpy()` their object representation into a byte array and back.
- Trivial types cannot be declared `const` without an initializer.
- When a trivial type is zero-initialized (for example, through value initialization {}), its data members will also be zero-initialized[17].

Let's try some code:

```
MyType0 t0{};
std::cout << t0.x << '\n';
MyType1 t1{};
std::cout << t1.x << '\n';
MyType2 t2{};
std::cout << t2.x << '\n';
MyType3 t3{};
std::cout << t3.x << '\n';
```

When you run the code @Compiler Explorer[18], you get the following output:

---

[16] https://timsong-cpp.github.io/cppwp/n4868/class.copy.ctor#11

[17] According to C++ Reference: The standard specifies that zero-initialization is not performed when the class has a user-provided or deleted default constructor, which implies that whether said default constructor is selected by overload resolution is not considered. All known compilers perform additional zero-initialization if a non-deleted defaulted default constructor is selected.

[18] https://godbolt.org/z/7bKnP6qea

```
0
408939456
0
0
```

As you can see, zero initialization kicks in, but not for `MyType1`. In that case, the compiler calls a default constructor but won't initialize the data member to `0`.

Similarly, for `const` variables:

```
// const MyType0 ct0; // error!
const MyType1 ct1; // fine, empty ctor called
// const MyType2 ct2; // error!
const MyType3 ct3; // fine
```

> ℹ️ Additionally, the class type is of *standard layout*, which essentially means that their memory layout is well defined and thus can be consumed by a C program. When a class is also trivial, sharing it across multiplatform code or communicating with the C code is easy. Read more at Trivial, standard-layout, POD, and literal types | Microsoft Docs[19].

> ℹ️ If you like to read more about trivial types, layout, and more, I highly recommend reading the book "Embracing Modern C++ Safely", chapter 2, page 401, "Generalized PODs".

Summary

While we completed the overview of regular constructors, move, copy, and even assignment operators. We can still learn more: see the next chapter on delegation and inheritance.

---

[19]https://docs.microsoft.com/en-us/cpp/cpp/trivial-standard-layout-and-pod-types?view=msvc-170

4. Delegating and Inheriting Constructors

In this chapter, we'll look at improvements from C++11 related to inheritance and the ability to call constructors from other constructors.

Delegating constructors

Sometimes, when your class contains many data members and several constructors, it might be convenient to reuse their initialization code. Fortunately, since C++11, you can use **delegating constructors**. Let's look at an example:

Ex 4.1. Delegating constructors. Run @Compiler Explorer

```cpp
class Product {
public:
    Product(int id, unsigned quantity, const std::string& name)
        : id_{id}, quantity_{quantity}, name_{name} { verifyData(); }
    explicit Product(const std::string& name) : Product{0, 0, name} { }
    void verifyData() {
        if (quantity_ > MaxQuantity)
            throw std::invalid_argument("quantity is too large!");
    }
    const std::string& name() const { return name_; }
private:
    int id_;
    unsigned quantity_;
    std::string name_;
    static constexpr unsigned MaxQuantity = 100;
};
```

In the above example, we declare two constructors. The first one performs the core job. The second calls the "primary" one. Inside this main constructor, we not only initialize data members but also call other code. In our case, it's a form of basic data validation.

And here's the demo code:

Ex 4.1. Delegating constructors, demo. Run @Compiler Explorer

```cpp
int main() {
    try {
        Product box{"a box"};
        std::cout << "product: " << box.name() << " created... \n";

        Product toy{101, 200, "a box"};
        std::cout << "product: " << toy.name() << " created... \n";
    }
    catch (const std::exception& e) {
        std::cout << "cannot create: " << e.what() << '\n';
    }
}
```

We can run it and get the following:

```
product: a box created...
cannot create: quantity is too large!
```

Without having delegating constructors, we'd have to duplicate the code:

```cpp
Product(int id, unsigned quantity, const std::string& name)
        : id_{id}, quantity_{quantity}, name_{name} {
    verifyData();
}
Product(const std::string& name, int id = 0)
    : id_{id}, quantity_{0}, name_{name} {
    verifyData();  // code duplication
}
```

As you can see, the code with the delegating constructor is much more compact and allows full code reuse. This saves typing and might eliminate various "copy&paste" bugs in your code.

What's more, the syntax doesn't limit us to regular constructors only, as you can call a constructor from a copy or move constructor:

```cpp
// copy:
Product(const Product& other) : Product{other.id_, other.quantity_, other.name_}
{ }
// move, potentially a bad idea (just for illustration)
Product(Product&& other)      : Product{other.id_, other.quantity_, other.name_}
{ }
```

In a case of a copy constructor, such code might reuse the validation parts. But, **be warned** about the move constructor, as the above code won't make any "moves" and will copy the data, which fails its primary purpose.

Be careful about the syntax!

`explicit PropertyInfo(double price) { PropertyInfo(...); }`

The above line will create a local object rather than calling the other constructor!
The call to a constructor has to appear before the constructor body.

Limitations

Writing too many constructors might lead to some mistakes and recursive calls. Take a look at the following code:

```cpp
class Product {
public:
    Product(int id, unsigned quantity, const std::string& name)
        : Product {name, id} { }
    explicit Product(const std::string& name, int id = 0)
        : Product{id, 0, name} { }
    // ...
};
Product recursion{"a single recursion"};
```

What happens when the `recursion` object calls its constructor?

You might get a segmentation fault and stack overflow! This is a recursive call, and the compiler cannot detect it until the code is executed at runtime.

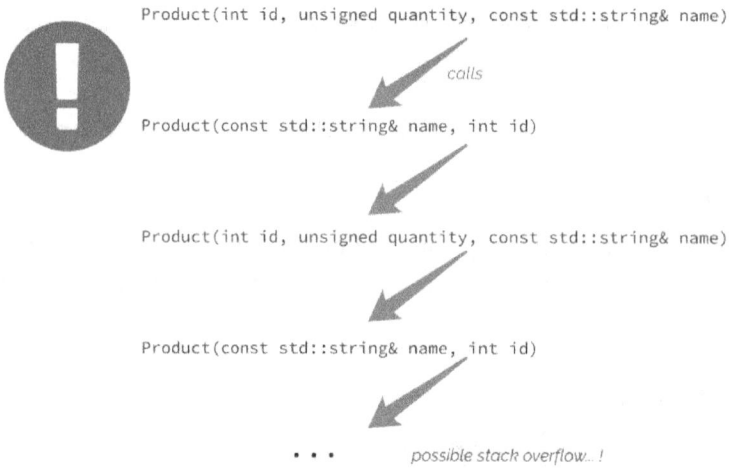

Another "restriction" is that you cannot mix member initialization with calling other constructors.

The following code won't compile:

```
Product(int id, unsigned quantity, const std::string& name)
        : Product {name, id}, quantity_{quantity} { }
```

For example, GCC reports the following error:

```
mem-initializer for 'Product::quantity_' follows constructor delegation
    7 |         : Product {name, id}, quantity_{quantity}
```

To sum up, if you want to use delegating constructors, you cannot initialize other data members.

Let's go to another section on constructors, where you'll learn one more modern C++ trick.

Inheritance

Let's look at situations where your class inherits from other classes. What happens with constructors? When does the compiler call them? This discussion will provide a background for a new feature from C++11 called *Inheriting Constructors*.

For debugging, let's introduce a derived class from `DataPacket` called `DebugData`, with special printing capabilities:

```cpp
class DebugDataPacket : public DataPacket {
public:
    DebugDataPacket(const std::string& name, size_t serverId)
     : DataPacket{name, serverId} { }

    void DebugPrint(std::ostream& os) {
        os << getData() << ", " << getCheckSum() << '\n';
    }
};
```

As you can see, the code declares a new class and uses : `public DataPacket` to indicate public inheritance. The example also defines a single constructor that invokes base class constructors.

C++ offers three options to specify the way we inherit from a base class:

- Public inheritance means that `public` members of the base class become `public` members of the derived class, and `protected` members are `protected` in the derived type.
- Protected inheritance makes all public and protected members of the base class accessible as protected members of the derived class.
- Private inheritance makes all public and protected base class members accessible as private members of the derived class.
- In all three cases, `private` members of the base class are not accessible by derived classes unless explicitly made `friend`.

We can use it like:

Ex 4.2. Inheritance, simple demo code. Run @Compiler Explorer

```cpp
int main() {
    DebugDataPacket hello{"hello!", 404};
    hello.DebugPrint(std::cout);
}
```

In the example, base class constructors are called explicitly. If there's no explicit call then each constructor will also call the default constructor of a base class implicitly. This is illustrated by the following code:

Ex 4.3. Base class construction order. Run @Compiler Explorer

```cpp
#include <iostream>
#include <string>

class Product {
public:
    Product() : id_{0} { std::cout << "Product() default\n"; }
    explicit Product(int id, const std::string& name)
        : id_{id}, name_{name} {
        std::cout << "Product(): " << id_ << ", " << name_ << '\n';
    }
protected:
    int id_;
    std::string name_;
};

class ExProduct : public Product {
public:
    ExProduct() { std::cout << "ExProduct() default\n"; }
    explicit ExProduct(int id) {
        id_ = id;
        std::cout << "ExProduct(id)\n";
    }
};

int main() {
    ExProduct p;
    ExProduct withId{42};
}
```

If we run the program, we'll get the following:

```
Product() default
ExProduct() default
Product() default
ExProduct(id)
```

As you can see, even though we haven't called any base constructor inside our ExProduct constructor, the compiler invoked it anyway. What's more, inside a constructor of a derived class, you cannot use base classes' data members in the initialization list, for example:

```
ExProduct(): id_(10) { // << err! We don't have access!
    std::cout << "ExProduct() default\n";
}
```

You can only access it in the body of the constructor:

```
ExProduct(int id) {
    id_ = id;
    std::cout << "ExProduct(id)\n";
}
```

This behavior is essential to keep the integrity of the object.

 Additionally, it's best not to call virtual functions in constructors as they might behave differently than expected. In short, a call to a virtual function in a base class constructor results in a call to the base implementation, as the inherited class and the implementation is not yet set up. You can read more about this behavior in the C++ FAQ[1] or at C++ Core Guideline C.82[2].

After introducing the inheritance topic, we can discuss one improvement we got with Modern C++.

Inheriting constructors

In our previous example with DebugPropertyInfo we didn't have any new data members, only some new member functions. The code showed a single constructor called the base class constructor. Since C++11, you can tell the compiler to "reuse" the code:

---

[1] https://isocpp.org/wiki/faq/strange-inheritance#calling-virtuals-from-ctors
[2] https://isocpp.github.io/CppCoreGuidelines/CppCoreGuidelines#Rc-ctor-virtual

Ex 4.4. Inheriting constructors. Run @Compiler Explorer

```cpp
class DebugDataPacket : public DataPacket {
public:
    using DataPacket::DataPacket;
    
    void DebugPrint(std::ostream& os) {
        os << getData() << ", " << getCheckSum() << '\n';
    }
};

int main() {
    DebugDataPacket hello{"hello!", 404};
    hello.DebugPrint(std::cout);
}
```

Consider **line 3**:

`using DataPacket::DataPacket;`

This tells the compiler that it can use **all** constructors from the base class, ignoring access modifiers. It means that all public constructors are visible and can be called, but the protected will still be `protected` in that context. See the example:

Ex 4.5. Inheriting constructors and protected section. Run @Compiler Explorer

```cpp
struct Base {
    int x{};
    int y{};
    Base(int a, int b): x{a}, y{b} { }
protected:
    Base() = default;
    Base(int a): x{a} { }
};

struct Derived : public Base {
    using Base::Base;
};
```

```
int main() {
    // Derived d{0};   // error: 'Base::Base(int)' is protected
    Derived d2{0, 1}; // fine
}
```

If you want to limit the access to constructors, you must explicitly write constructors for `Derived`:

```
Derived(int a) : Base{a} { }

Derived d{0}; // fine now, as Derived::Derived(int) is public
```

Summary

Now that we have covered all the details about constructors, it's important to address a strictly-linked topic: destructors. Destructors play a crucial role in object lifecycle management and allow us to clean up resources. See the next chapter to get more details.

5. Destructors

While constructors are responsible for various situations where an object is created, C++ also offers a way to handle object destruction. C++ doesn't provide any form of garbage collection available in many popular programming languages, but thanks to precise lifetime specification, you can be confident when your object will be destroyed.

Each class has a special member function called a destructor. If you don't write one, the compiler prepares a default implementation. A destructor is called when an object ends its lifetime. In most cases, it means that an object goes out of scope (for stack-allocated variables), or when a delete operator is called (for heap-allocated variables). Additionally, when you have a user-defined class, it will automatically call destructors for its data members (in the reverse declaration order) For more information about lifetime, see a good summary at C++Reference page[1].

Basics

Before we move on, we should expand our terminology. So far, I mentioned "object" to refer to entities of some type and relied on our "intuition" to access such entities. But the C++ Standard defines an *object* in the following terms (simplified, based on C++ Draft - intro.object[2]):

> The constructs in a C++ program create, destroy, refer to, access, and manipulate objects. An object is created by a definition, by a new-expression, by an operation that implicitly creates objects, or when a temporary object is created. An object occupies a region of storage in its period of construction, throughout its lifetime, and in its period of destruction.

And continuing:

---
[1]https://en.cppreference.com/w/cpp/language/lifetime
[2]https://timsong-cpp.github.io/cppwp/n4868/intro.object#1

> - An object can have a name,
> - An object has a storage duration which influences its lifetime,
> - An object has a type,
> - Objects can contain other objects, called subobjects. A subobject can be a member subobject, a base class subobject, or an array element.

Here's a basic scenario for a destructor that handles a case where the lifetime of an object ends:

Ex 5.1. A logging destructor. Run @Compiler Explorer

```cpp
#include <iostream>
#include <string>

class Product {
public:
    explicit Product(const char* name, unsigned id)
    : name_(name), id_(id) {
        std::cout << name << ", id " << id << '\n';
    }
    ~Product() { std::cout << name_ << " destructor...\n"; }

    std::string name() const { return name_; }
    unsigned id() const { return id_; }
private:
    std::string name_;
    unsigned id_;
};
```

The example contains the following special member function:

```cpp
~Product() { std::cout << name_ << " destructor...\n"; }
```

The syntax is unique as it has no parameters and has the ~ prefix. You can also have only one destructor in a class. What's more, a destructor doesn't return any value.

Now, let's create two objects of that type:

Ex 5.1. A logging destructor, continuation. Run @Compiler Explorer

```
int main() {
    {
        Product tvset("TV Set", 123);
    }
    {
        Product car("Mustang", 999);
    }
}
```

In our case, the constructor and the destructor are used to perform the logging. When you run the example, you'll see the following output:

```
TV Set, id 123
TV Set destructor...
Mustang, id 999
Mustang destructor...
```

I specifically enclosed objects (created on the stack) in separate scopes so that their lifetime ends when their scope ends. On the other hand, if we have code:

```
int main() {
    Product tvset("TV Set", 123);
    Product car("Mustang", 999);
}
```

Then both `tvset` and `car` share the same lifetime scope so that we can expect the following output:

```
TV Set, id 123
Mustang, id 999
Mustang destructor...
TV Set destructor..
```

As you can see, the destructors are called in the reverse order of how they were created. It's because the stack is a LIFO structure (Last In, First Out). `tvset` was created first and added to the stack, then car is added. When the function goes out of scope, the stack is cleared, taking elements in reverse order. So car is deleted first, and then tvset. This is illustrated by the following diagram:

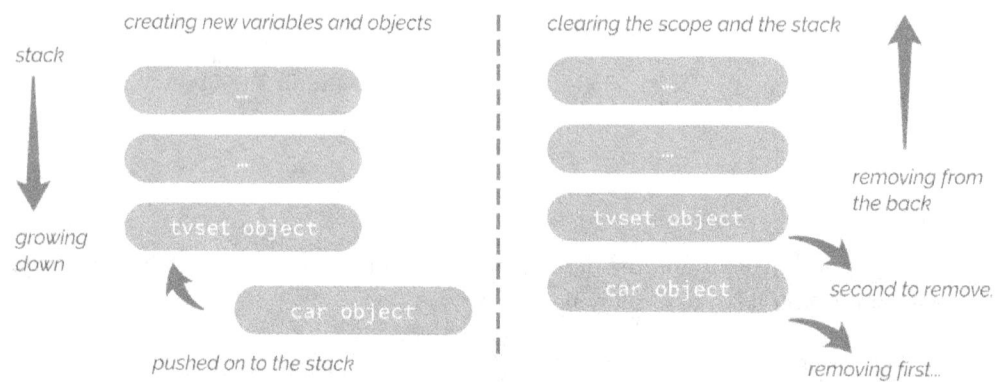

Adding and removing objects from the stack.

Objects allocated on the heap

In the previous examples, I used objects created on the stack. For a clearer picture of destructors, it's good to discuss a case when you have objects on the heap. In that case, a destructor will be called only when the memory is released via the delete operator.

Consider the following snippet:

```
{
    Product* ptr = new Product("TV Set", 123);
}
// !!
```

ptr is a pointer to an object allocated on the heap. But I didn't call delete, and thus, the destructor won't be invoked! Moreover, I generated a memory leak since the memory was also not released. After the scope ends, ptr goes out of the scope, but since it's a pointer, the memory is still present but not accessible.

To fix the issue we have to call delete (for single elements) or delete [] (for arrays).

```cpp
{
    Product* ptr = new Product("TV Set", 123);
    // use ptr...
    delete ptr;
}
```

And similarly, for an array:

```cpp
{
    Product* arr = new Product[10]("TV Set", 123);
    // use...
    delete [] arr;
}
```

Since it's easy to forget about proper heap release, it's best to use smart pointers that wrap allocation with the ownership.

```cpp
{
    std::unique_ptr<Product> ptr = std::make_unique<Product>("box", 1);
    // use ptr...
}
```

Now, when `ptr` goes out of the scope, it's "smart" and knows it also has to call `delete` on the stored pointer. In the example, I'm using a `unique_ptr` as the basic form of smart pointers in the C++ Standard Library. It wraps the pointer to an object and keeps the "unique" ownership of it. If you want to pass pointers around in the system and have multiple "owners," then you can use `shared_ptr`.

The smart pointer will also work for the array version:

```cpp
{
    // create 10 Products
    std::unique_ptr<Product[]> ptr = std::make_unique<Product[]>(10);
    // use...
}
```

And this time, the `unique_ptr` makes sure the `delete []` is called. You can play with the example @Compiler Explorer[3].

---

[3] https://godbolt.org/z/Ps9Ye79zc

For more information about smart pointers, have a look at my blog series: 6 Ways to Refactor new/delete into unique ptr - C++ Stories[4] and more articles about smart pointers @C++Stories[5].

 What's more, Modern C++ strongly suggests avoiding raw `new` and `delete`. Thanks to many library containers, wrappers, and smart pointers, there's almost no need to rely on those low-level memory management routines. See this C++ Core Guideline: R.11: Avoid calling `new` and `delete` explicitly[6]. The code in this section with `new` can be treated only for illustrative purpose.

Destructors and data members

By default, parent classes' destructor calls the destructors for all data members in the reverse declaration order:

Ex 5.2. A nested destructor call. Run @Compiler Explorer

```
#include <iostream>
#include <string>

class Product {
    // defined as in the previous example...
};

class Wrapper {
public:
    Wrapper() : prod_("internal", 123) { std::cout << "Wrapper()\n"; }
    ~Wrapper() { std::cout << "~Wrapper()\n"; }
private:
    Product prod_;
};

int main() {
    Wrapper w;
}
```

---

[4]https://www.cppstories.com/2021/refactor-into-uniqueptr/
[5]https://www.cppstories.com/tags/smart-pointers/
[6]https://isocpp.github.io/CppCoreGuidelines/CppCoreGuidelines#r11-avoid-calling-new-and-delete-explicitly

In example 5.2, the `Wrapper` class contains `Product` as a data member.

The output:

```
internal, id 123
Wrapper()
~Wrapper()
internal destructor...
```

As you notice, `internal destructor` is called along with the `~Wrapper()` invocation.

On the other hand, when your object is part of some other class as a pointer, it will go out of the scope but not the data it points to. So you have to pay attention to your pointer data members and call their `delete` in a proper place. See an example below:

Ex 5.3. A pointer data member and a destructor. Run @Compiler Explorer

```cpp
class Wrapper {
public:
    Wrapper() : prod_(new Product("internal", 123)) {
        std::cout << "Wrapper()\n";
    }
    ~Wrapper() {
        delete prod_;
        std::cout << "~Wrapper()\n";
    }
private:
    Product *prod_;
};

int main() {
    Wrapper w;
}
```

This time I had to manually call `delete prod_` to release the data member properly. It's another case where a smart pointer is handy as it will automatically destroy the underlying object.

Virtual destructors and polymorphism

There's also one feature of destructors that plays an essential part in inheritance and polymorphism.

According to Wikipedia[7]:

> In programming language theory and type theory, polymorphism is the provision of a single interface to entities of different types or the use of a single symbol to represent multiple different types.

In C++, the definition means that if you have a pointer or a reference to a base class, and when you call a `virtual` member function, the compiler invokes an implementation (if available) in the derived classes. C++ does this technique through `virtual` functions. We can demonstrate it with the following but naïve code in C++:

Ex 5.4. Virtual destructor, base class, incorrect. Run @Compiler Explorer

```
class Product {
public:
    explicit Product(const char* name) : name_(name) {
        std::cout << name << '\n';
    }
    ~Product() { std::cout << name_ << " destructor...\n"; }

    std::string name() const { return name_; }
    virtual double calculateMass() const = 0;
private:
    std::string name_;
};
```

The above `Product` type declares a `virtual` member function. We can declare derived classes and then provide their implementation of that virtual member function. This allows the compiler to call the proper function based on the type and give this "polymorphic" semantics.

Have a look:

---

[7]https://en.wikipedia.org/wiki/Polymorphism_(computer_science)

Ex 5.4. Virtual destructor, derived classes. Run @Compiler Explorer

```cpp
struct BoxProduct : public Product {
    using Product::Product; // inheriting ctor
    ~BoxProduct() { std::cout << "~BoxProduct...\n"; }
    double calculateMass() const override { return 10.0; }
};

struct FluidProduct : public Product {
    using Product::Product; // inheriting ctor
    ~FluidProduct() { std::cout << "~FluidProduct...\n"; }
    double calculateMass() const override { return 100.0; }
};
```

The CalculateMass function has two separate and trivial implementations[8]. The function signature also uses the override keyword, which is a C++11 addition. It tells the compiler that a given member function is about to be overridden, so the compiler can check if there's a corresponding declaration in a base class. Read more about the keyword in my article: Modern C++: Safety and Expressiveness with override and final @C++Stories[9].

We can now write code that uses both of those products:

Ex 5.4. Virtual destructor, main. Run @Compiler Explorer

```cpp
void CallCalculate(const Product& prod) {
    std::cout << "calculating: " << prod.calculateMass() << '\n';
}

int main() {
    using std::unique_ptr;
    using std::make_unique;
    unique_ptr<Product> box = make_unique<BoxProduct>("box");
    unique_ptr<Product> water = make_unique<FluidProduct>("water");
    CallCalculate(*box.get());
    CallCalculate(*water.get());
}
```

---

[8]Let's assume that in the actual production code, those functions would have some more advanced calculations based on the properties of a particular type.

[9]https://www.cppstories.com/2021/override-final/

The demo use case is simple, it creates two smart pointers that are pointers to a base class, but they are assigned with pointers to derived classes. When we run the code @Compiler Explorer[10], you'll see the following output:

```
box
water
calculating: 10
calculating: 100
water destructor...
box destructor...
```

As you can see, the `CallCalculate(Product& prod)` function takes a reference to a base class, and then it can call its functions. If a function is virtual, the compiler will call it polymorphically based on the real type.

But... do you see an error here?

Take a moment and think...

It looks like the destructor of the derived class is not called!

This is because we used pointers to hold our objects. And when the smart pointer goes out of the scope, it will call `delete` on the pointer to a base class. Since the destructor is not marked as `virtual`, the polymorphism doesn't kick in, and only the `~Product()` destructor is called and not the derived one.

To fix this, each class that has virtual functions should also have a virtual destructor:

```cpp
virtual ~Product() {
    std::cout << name_ << " destructor...\n";
}
```

This fixes our output:

---

[10]https://godbolt.org/z/cb9Pfhhqe

```
box
water
calculating: 10
calculating: 100
~FluidProduct...
water destructor...
~BoxProduct...
box destructor...
```

You can play with the correct example @Compiler Explorer[11].

There's also a specific C++ Core Guideline related to this critical aspect. See C.35: A base class destructor should be either public and virtual, or protected and non-virtual[12]:

> **Reason**: To prevent undefined behavior. If the destructor is public, then the calling code can attempt to destroy a derived class object through a base class pointer, and the result is undefined if the base class's destructor is non-virtual.

Partially created objects

The compiler calls a destructor only for objects that are fully created. Consider the modified version of a constructor that checks the `id` parameter and throws an exception:

```cpp
explicit Product(const char* name, unsigned id) : name_(name), id_(id) {
    std::cout << name << ", id " << id << '\n';
    if (id < 100)
        throw std::runtime_error{"bad id..."};
}
```

---

[11]https://godbolt.org/z/dfa49sjc6
[12]https://isocpp.github.io/CppCoreGuidelines/CppCoreGuidelines#c35-a-base-class-destructor-should-be-either-public-and-virtual-or-protected-and-non-virtual

Ex 5.5. Destructors and partial object creation. Run @Compiler Explorer

```
int main() {
    try {
        Product tvset("TV Set", 123);
        Product car("Mustang", 9);
    }
    catch (const std::exception& ex) {
        std::cout << "exception: " << ex.what() << '\n';
    }
}
```

When we run the example, we'll get the output:

```
TV Set, id 123
Mustang, id 9
TV Set destructor...
exception: bad id...
```

This time the example creates two objects: `TV set` and `Mustang`. In the output, we can notice that both objects call their constructors, but there's only one destructor invocation (for `TV set`). Since `Mustang` threw an exception in the constructor, the destructor won't be executed.

 Since destructors might be called when the compiler performs stack unwinding, they shouldn't throw exceptions, as this might result in calling `std::terminate()`. Read this C++ Core Guideline suggestion for more information: E.16: Destructors, deallocation, and swap must never fail[13].

Another important aspect is to manage resources allocated before the exception occurs properly. For example, if you allocate some memory dynamically using a raw pointer, you might get a memory leak. See the following sample:

---

[13]https://isocpp.github.io/CppCoreGuidelines/CppCoreGuidelines#Re-never-fail

Ex 5.6. A memory leak in partially created objects. Run @Compiler Explorer

```cpp
class Product {
public:
    explicit Product(int id) : res_(new Resource()) {
        std::cout << "Product: id " << id << '\n';
        if (id < MIN_ID)
            throw std::runtime_error{"bad id..."};
    }
    ~Product() {
        delete res_;
        std::cout <<  "~Product...\n";
    }
private:
    Resource* res_;
};

int main() {
    try {
        Product invalid(MIN_ID - 1);
    }
    catch (const std::exception& ex) {
        std::cout << "exception: " << ex.what() << '\n';
    }
}
```

The output:

```
Product: id 99
exception: bad id...
```

As you can see, the compiler didn't call the destructor for `Resource`, and the memory wasn't released (since we called : `res_(new Resource())` in the constructor). We could fix this leak by deleting `res_` before we throw. Still, manual resource management is fragile, and it's best to look for a better solution.

The key mechanism to fix such leaking resources is to rely on variables and data members with automatic storage duration, like regular value types. In that case, the stack unwinding destroys them properly and calls their destructors. That's why a destructor for smart pointers can be safely called:

Ex 5.7. Fixing memory leaks in partially created objects. Run @Compiler Explorer

```cpp
class Product {
public:
    explicit Product(int id) : res_(std::make_unique<Resource>()) {
        std::cout << "Product: id " << id << '\n';
        if (id < MIN_ID)
            throw std::runtime_error{"bad id..."};
    }
    ~Product() {
        std::cout <<  "~Product...\n";
    }
private:
    std::unique_ptr<Resource> res_; // << smart pointer now!
};

int main() {
    try {
        Product invalid(MIN_ID - 1);
    }
    catch (const std::exception& ex) {
        std::cout << "exception: " << ex.what() << '\n';
    }
}
```

When we run the code, we'll see the following output:

```
Product: id 99
~Resource
exception: bad id...
```

The compiler didn't call the destructor for `Product`, but the stack unwinding correctly called the destructor for all data members.

 You can read more information about stack unwinding and handling resources on the following sites: throw expression - @C++Reference[14] and Exceptions and Error Handling, C++ FAQ[15].

---

[14]https://en.cppreference.com/w/cpp/language/throw#Stack_unwinding
[15]https://isocpp.org/wiki/faq/exceptions#selfcleaning-members

A compiler-generated destructor

As with other special member functions, the compiler creates an implicit default destructor for your classes if you don't provide your implementation. The basic rule is that each data member and also the base classes must have an accessible destructor (they are not deleted, not inaccessible, nor ambiguous). For example:

Ex 5.8. Compiler-generated destructor. Run @C++Insights

```cpp
#include <iostream>
#include <string>

class Product {
public:
    explicit Product(int id, const std::string& name)
        : id_(id), name_(name) {
        std::cout << "Product(): " << id_ << ", " << name_ << '\n';
    }
private:
    int id_;
    std::string name_;
};

int main() {
    Product first{10, "basic"};
}
```

At C++Insights, we can see the output from the compiler and how it "sees" the code. As you can notice, the compiler created the following destructor for us:

```cpp
inline ~Product() noexcept = default;
```

You can read more about compiler-generated destructors in the "Implicitly-declared destructor" section @C++Reference[16].

---
[16]https://en.cppreference.com/w/cpp/language/destructor

Summary

This chapter covered a destructor, a special member functions invoked when an object ends its lifetime. In most cases, we can use this capability to properly clean up the object and deallocate any resources we have used and have yet to release.

For example, you allocate some memory when the object is created, and then the memory must be released to avoid memory leaks. Similarly, you can open a file or a database connection, and then you must ensure the file or the connection is closed when the object goes out of scope.

Destructors are one of the best features of the C++ language as they provide a clear and well-defined point at where they are called. This is opposed to dynamic garbage collection that can work in the background, potentially slowing down the program and with less control over the process. Destructors are also the critical element to a popular term in C++ called RAII (Resource Acquisition is Initialization), coined by B. Stroustrup, the author of the C++ language. It states that holding a resource is a class invariant, and is tied to the object's lifetime. Read more at Wikipedia[17].

Fortunately, in Modern C++, there are fewer and fewer places where you need custom destructors. For example, when your data members are standard containers (like `std::vector<int>`, or `std::map<std::string, int>`) in your classes, then you can rely on default destructors to do the job. Standard containers like `std::vector<int>` might allocate memory buffers, but they also manage that buffer and release it properly, so you don't need to take any action when using them in a class.

---

[17]https://en.wikipedia.org/wiki/Resource_acquisition_is_initialization

6. Type Deduction and Initialization

Since C++11, we can write shorter code thanks to automatic type inference with `auto` or `decltype` keywords. Rather than specifying the full type for a new object, we can ask the compiler to deduce its type. But that's not all, as in C++17, we got even more handy features related to type deduction. That's why in this chapter, we'll learn about the following:

- How "type deduction" affects initialization,
- `auto` and `decltype` rules,
- Structured bindings from C++17,
- Class Type Argument Deduction (CTAD), also from C++17,

Near the end, we'll also discuss the "AAA" rule - Almost Always Auto. Let's start!

Deduction with `auto`

One of the most prominent cases where `auto` helps is when you work with iterators or other "verbose" types. Before C++11, you had to specify the exact type of the iterator:

```cpp
std::map<std::string, int> mapping { ... };
std::map<std::string, int>::iterator it = mapping.find("hello");

std::vector<std::pair<int, double>> pairs { ... };
std::vector<std::pair<int, double>>::const_iterator startIT = pairs.cbegin();
```

Since C++11, you can ask the compiler to deduce the correct type (at compile time):

```cpp
auto it = mapping.find("hello");
auto startIT = pairs.cbegin();
```

Type deduction is also a lifesaver for cases with maps:

Ex 6.1. Trying a correct type for map elements. Run @Compiler Explorer

```
map<string, int> m { {"hello", 1}, {"world", 2}};

for (const pair<string, int>& elem : m)
    cout << elem.first << ", " << &elem.first << '\n';

cout << m.begin()->first << ", " << &m.begin()->first << '\n';
cout << next(m.begin())->first << ", " << &next(m.begin())->first << '\n';
```

Do you see the problem here? If you run the program, you'll see the following addresses:

```
hello, 0x7ffe4eb027f0 // loop iteration 1
world, 0x7ffe4eb027f0 // loop iteration 2
hello, 0x15ae2d0
world, 0x15ae320
```

We have a mismatch! `std::pair<std::string, int>` is not the correct type when iterating through `std::map`. The proper type is `std::pair<const std::string, int>`. In other words, the key has to be constant. Since the type differs, the compiler has to create copies for `elem` (it performs an implicit conversion)! When you replace the loop line with:

```
for (const auto& elem : m) // or...
for (const std::pair<const std::string, int>& elem : m)
```

The code compiles and produces exact addresses. For example:

```
hello, 0x7c32d0 // loop iteration 1
world, 0x7c3320 // loop iteration 2
hello, 0x7c32d0
world, 0x7c3320
```

In some cases, we don't even know the type. This happens for lambdas, where the compiler creates some unique, anonymous name for the type of each lambda (the so-called "closure type"):

```
auto fooSquare = [](int x) { return x*x; }
```

Before we see all rules for `auto` and its friends, let's look at one crucial topic in C++: value categories.

About value categories in C++

Value categories are a way to classify expressions into different categories based on the kind of object they represent and how they behave. Knowing about those categories will help us discuss features that relate to initialization. As of C++20, we have three main value categories:

Lvalue: An expression representing an object with a persistent memory address, such as a named object or an object accessed through an lvalue reference.

For example:

```
int x = 5;
x = 6;    // x is an lvalue, and can be modified
```

Xvalue: An expression that represents a temporary object, such as the result of a function that returns by value or an object that's about to be moved from.

```
std::string hello { "Hello"}; // hello is an lvalue
static_cast<int&&>(hello);    // this expression is an xvalue
```

Prvalue: An expression whose evaluation initializes an object or a bit-field, or computes the value of the operand of an operator, as specified by the context in which it appears.

```
int x = 5 + 6;   // 5 + 6 is a prvalue expression
int y = 42;      // y is lvalue, 42 is prvalue
nullptr;         // nullptr is prvalue
```

And if an expression is *prvalue* or *xvalue* we say it's an *rvalue*.

See more at Value categories @C++ Reference[1] and Value categories, and references to them @Microsoft Learn[2].

Now, let's see the core principles for `auto`.

---

[1] https://en.cppreference.com/w/cpp/language/value_category#xvalue
[2] https://learn.microsoft.com/en-us/windows/uwp/cpp-and-winrt-apis/cpp-value-categories

Rules for `auto` type deduction

We can summarize the rules for `auto` in the following list of five cases:

1. If the initializer is a constant expression, the type of the variable is deduced to be the type of the expression:

```cpp
auto num = 42;     // num is an int
auto pi = 3.14;    // pi is double
auto str = "hello world";   // str is const char*
auto p = nullptr;            // p is std::nullptr_t
```

2. If the initializer is an expression with a type that is not a reference, the type of the variable is deduced to be the type of the expression, with top-level cv-qualifiers (`const` or `volatile` qualifiers) removed:

```cpp
int num = 42;
const int cnum = num;
const int* pNum = &num;
const int* const pCNum = &num;
```

Using direct list initialization:

```cpp
auto a { num };      // a is int
auto a2 { cnum };    // a2 is int, const removed
auto a3 { pNum };    // a3 is const int*
auto a4 { pCNum };   // a4 is const int*, const removed
```

The same deduction happens when you use copy initialization syntax:

```cpp
auto b = num;      // b is int
auto b2 = cnum;    // b2 is int, const removed
auto b3 = pNum;    // b3 is const int*
auto b4 = pCnum;   // b4 is const int*, const removed
```

3. If the initializer is an expression with a type that is a reference, the type of the variable is deduced to be the type of the referred-to object, with top-level cv-qualifiers and references removed:

```cpp
int num = 42;
int& rnum = num;
const int& crnum = num;

auto c { num };     // c is int
auto c2 { rnum };   // c2 is int, ref removed
auto c3 { crnum };  // c3 is int, const and ref removed
auto d = num;       // d is int
auto d2 = rnum;     // d2 is int, ref removed
auto d3 = crnum;    // d3 is int, const and ref removed
```

4. If the initialization is copy-list-initialization, the type of the variable is deduced to be a **std::initializer_list** of the appropriate type:

```cpp
auto list = { 1, 2, 3}; // list is std::initializer_list<int>
auto one = { 1.1 };     // one is std::initializer_list<double>
```

Notice that copy initialization gives different results than copy list initialization:

```cpp
auto x { 42 };     // direct list initialization, x is int
auto y = 42;       // copy initialization, y is int
auto z = { 42 };   // copy list initialization, z is initializer_list<int>!
```

5. If the initializer is a lambda expression, the type of the variable is deduced to be a unique, unnamed closure type:

```cpp
auto magic = [](){}; // magic has type unique, unnamed callable type
int num = 10;
auto mulByNum = [&num](int y) { return num*y; }
```

Adding type specifiers

You can also add a reference, **const** or a pointer signature to force concrete types:

```cpp
int num = 42;
auto& ref = num;             // ref is int&
const auto& cref = num;      // cref is const int&
auto* pNum = &num;           // pNum is int*
```

There's also a special type specifier, `auto&&` that can bind to lvalues and rvalues and preserves the constness:

```cpp
std::string hello { "Hello" };
std::string& refHello = hello;
auto&& str = hello;          // str is string&
auto&& rstr = refHello;      // rstr is string&

const std::string world { "World" };
const std::string& refWorld = world;
auto&& w = world;            // w is const string&
auto&& rw = refWorld;        // rw is const string&
```

The above example shows a basic use of `auto&&` (also called universal or forwarding reference[3]). In the case of `str` or `rstr`, the deduced type is a reference to `std::string`. In a case where the initializer is a constant, the resulting reference will also be `const`; see `w` and `rw`. There's also an interesting property that `auto&&` can bind to rvalue references ("temporaries"):

```cpp
// auto& str2 = std::string { "HI" }; // err! can bind to lvalues only!
const auto& str3 = std::string { "HI"}; // fine, but const ref
//str3[1] = 'i';                        // err, it's const
auto&& str4 = std::string { "HI" }; // fine! str4 is string&&
str4[1] = 'i';                       // fine to change
```

The line with `str3` generates a compiler error, while the other two lines are fine. The main difference is that `str3` is a constant object. `auto&&` (in `str4`) is more flexible. It's an essential part of the range-based for loop so that it can work with containers that are constant or not.

---

[3]See more about universal references in this amazing article by Scott Meyers: https://isocpp.org/blog/2012/11/universal-references-in-c11-scott-meyers.

Another view on the deduction

Conceptually, when you write `/*qualifiers*/ auto x = expr;` the compiler uses the same rules as for template type deduction:

```
template <typename T> x_func(/*qualifiers*/ T param) { }
x_func(/*expr*/);
```

In an amazing book by Scott Meyers - "Effective Modern C++", Item 2 - we can read about three following cases:

1. The type specifier is a pointer or a reference but not a universal reference

```
int num = 42;
const auto& rx = num;
// same deduction as:
template <typename T> foo_rx(const T& num) { };
foo_rx(num);
```

Above, we can see that the code for deducing type `rx` involves the same rules as passing `num` to `foo_rx`.

2. The type specifier is a universal reference

```
auto&& ux = 42;
template <typename T> foo_ux(T&& num) { };
foo_ux(42);
```

3. The type specifier is neither a pointer nor a reference.

```
auto num = 42;
template <typename T> foo_num(T num) { };
foo_num(42);
```

Let's meet the second keyword from C++11, `decltype`.

Deduction with `decltype`

The `decltype` keyword is used to determine the type of a variable or expression based on its declaration. If you use `decltype` on a variable (or a member), it will return the type of that variable (or a member), including any `const` or reference qualifiers. For example:

```cpp
int x = 10;
decltype(x) y = 20; // y is int
const int z = 30;
decltype(z) w = 40; // w is const int
```

While `auto` strips away `const` and reference qualifiers, `decltype` returns the exact type of the variable or expression. Another difference is that `decltype` can be used on expressions and variables, while `auto` can only be used on initializers. You can use `decltype` to determine the type of more complex expressions, such as function calls or template arguments. For example:

```cpp
template <typename T, typename U>
auto foo(T x, U y) -> decltype(x + y) { return x + y; }
```

Above, we don't know the types of the template parameters, and the result of the + operator might not be the same as T or U. `decltype` combined with trailing return type (C++11) gives us more freedom, especially for generic code.

In short, if the argument for decltype is an unparenthesized expression, we have three cases:

1. if the value category of expression is xvalue, then `decltype` yields T&&,
2. if the value category of expression is lvalue, then `decltype` yields T&,
3. if the value category of expression is prvalue, then `decltype` yields T,

For example:

```cpp
std::string name { "a funny name" };
// decltype(name) is std::string -> exact name of a variable
// decltype((name)) is std::string& -> parenthesized
struct Object { int x; std::string n; };
const Object obj { 0, "" };
// decltype(obj) is const Object -> exact name of a variable
// decltype(obj.x) is int -> data member expression
```

If the variable is parenthesized, the argument is treated as an lvalue expression:

```
int x = 10;
decltype(x) y = 10; // y is also int
decltype((x)) z = y; // z is int& !
```

One handy use case for `decltype` is declaring a proper return type for a function based on the type of the function's parameters:

Ex 6.2. decltype and return type. Run @Compiler Explorer

```
struct Object {
    int& param() { return val; }
    int val { 0 };
};
auto forwardParam(Object& obj) -> decltype(obj.param()) {
    return obj.param();
}
int main() {
    Object x;
    forwardParam(x) = 42;
}
```

In the above example, `decltype` is used to get the return type of a member function from the `Object` class. The function returns precisely the same type, including its cv-qualifiers, as the `param()` member function.

Additionally, since C++14, you can shorten the function declaration, use `decltype(auto)`, and don't write trailing return type.

```
decltype(auto) forwardParam(Object& obj) {
    return obj.param();
}
```

Note that the function returns a reference, and that's why we can change the value of `x.val`. If we used `auto` for return type deduction, we wouldn't get a proper value category (it would strip the reference).

Printing type info

With some extra machinery[4], we can run an experiment and show the types of our variables:

Ex 6.3. Printing type info. Run @Compiler Explorer

```
template <typename T>
constexpr std::string_view typeName()  {
    constexpr auto prefix = std::string_view{"with T = "};
    constexpr auto function = std::string_view{__PRETTY_FUNCTION__};
    const auto start = function.find(prefix) + prefix.size();
    return function.substr(start, function.find("; ") - start);
}

template <typename T, typename... Ts>
void typeNames(const char*str ) {
    std::cout << str << typeName<T>();
    ((std::cout << ", " << typeName<Ts>()), ...); // fold expression, C++17
}
```

The code uses the `__PRETTY_FUNCTION__` compile-time string. It slices it in predefined places to extract the template parameter typename. Later this function is applied on the variadic pack inside `typeNames()`, and the names are printed via `std::cout`.

And here's an example:

Ex 6.3. Printing type info, use cases. Run @Compiler Explorer

```
int main() {
    int num = 42;
    int& rnum = num;
    const int& crnum = num;

    auto c { num };
    auto c2 { rnum };
    auto c3 { crnum };
    typeNames<decltype(c), decltype(c2), decltype(c3)>("c, c2, c3: ");
    typeNames<decltype((c)), decltype((c2))>("\n(c), (c2): ");
```

[4]Using GCC's `__PRETTY_FUNCTION__` based on https://stackoverflow.com/questions/281818/unmangling-the-result-of-stdtypeinfoname. Solutions based on `typeid()` might not work, as they don't convey CV qualifiers as `decltype()` does.

```cpp
    auto x { 42 };        // x is int
    auto y = 42;          // y is int
    auto z = { 42 };      // z is initializer_list<int>!
    typeNames<decltype(x), decltype(y), decltype(z)>("\nx, y, z: ");
    typeNames<decltype((x)), decltype((y))>("\n(x), (y): ");

    struct Object { std::string str; };
    const Object unknown { "unknown" };
    const Object& refunknown = unknown;
    auto&& u = unknown;
    auto&& refu = refunknown;
    typeNames<decltype(u), decltype(refu)>("\nu and refu: ");
}
```

The output:

```
c, c2, c3: int, int, int
(c), (c2): int&, int&
x, y, z: int, int, std::initializer_list<int>
(x), (y): int&, int&
u and refu: const main()::Object&, const main()::Object&
```

The program shows the type names from three groups of `auto` use cases. By using `decltype` we can precisely get the types and preserve their constness or reference status. Additionally, we have the output for parenthesized options that gives lvalue expressions.

Thanks to `auto`, we can declare variables, and there's no need to spell their long type names. But in C++17, we also got another cool addition. Let's meet structured bindings.

Structured bindings since C++17

Starting from C++17, you can write:

```cpp
std::set<int> mySet;
auto [iter, inserted] = mySet.insert(10);
```

`insert()` returns `std::pair` indicating if the element was inserted or not, and the iterator to this element. Instead of `pair.first` and `pair.second`, you can use variables with concrete names[5].

Such syntax is called a *structured binding expression*.

The Syntax

The basic syntax for structured bindings is as follows:

```cpp
auto [a, b] = expression;
auto [a, b, c] { expression };
auto [a, b, c, d] ( expression );
```

The compiler introduces all identifiers from the `a, b, c, d` (you can specify more variables if you need, of course) as names in the surrounding scope and binds them to sub-objects or elements of the object denoted by the expression.

Behind the scenes, the compiler might generate the following **pseudo code** (assuming a tuple with three elements):

```cpp
auto temp = expression;
using a = tempTuple.first;
using b = tempTuple.second;
using c = tempTuple.third;
```

Conceptually, the expression is copied (or a new object is created) into a hidden/unnamed object (`temp`) with member variables that are exposed through a, b and c. However, the

---

[5]you can also assign the result to your variables by using `std::tie()`; still, this technique is not as convenient as structured bindings in C++17.

variables a, b, and c are not references; they are aliases (or bindings) to the generated object member variables. We can also say they are merely names for the members of the unnamed main object[6]. The "hidden" object has a unique name assigned by the compiler.

For example:

```
std::pair a(0, 1.0f);
auto [x, y] = a;
```

x binds to `int` stored in the generated object that is a copy of a. And similarly, y binds to `float`.

Modifiers

Several modifiers can be used with structured bindings:

`const` modifiers:

```
const auto [a, b, c] = expression;
```

References:

```
auto& [a, b, c] = expression;
auto&& [a, b, c] = expression;
```

For example:

```
std::pair a(0, 1.0f);
auto& [x, y] = a;
x = 10;  // write access
// a.first is now 10
```

In the example, x binds to the element in the generated object, which is a reference to a.

Now it's also relatively easy to get a reference to a tuple member:

---

[6]Thanks to Timur Doumler for pointing this out.

```cpp
auto& [ refA, refB, refC, refD ] = myTuple;
```

Or better via a `const` reference:

```cpp
const auto& [ refA, refB, refC, refD ] = myTuple;
```

You can also add `[[attribute]]` to structured bindings:

```cpp
[[maybe_unused]] auto& [a, b, c] = expression;
```

Binding

Structured Binding is not only limited to tuples; we have three cases from which we can bind from:

1. If the initializer is an array:

```cpp
// works with arrays:
double myArray[3] = { 1.0, 2.0, 3.0 };
auto [a, b, c] = myArray;
```

In this case, an array is copied into a temporary object, and a, b, and c refers to copied elements from the array.

The number of identifiers must match the number of elements in the array.

2. If the initializer supports `std::tuple_size<>`, provides `get<N>()` and also exposes `std::tuple_element` functions:

```cpp
std::pair myPair(0, 1.0f);
auto [a, b] = myPair; // binds myPair.first/second
```

In the above snippet, we bind to `myPair`. But this also means you can provide support for your classes, assuming you add the `get<N>` interface implementation. See an example in the later section.

3. If the initializer's type contains only non-static data members:

```cpp
struct Point  { double x;   double y; };
Point GetStartPoint() { return { 0.0, 0.0 }; }

const auto [x, y] = GetStartPoint();
```

x and y refer to `Point::x` and `Point::y` from the `Point` structure.

The class doesn't have to be POD, but the number of identifiers must equal to the number of non-static data members. The members must also be accessible from the given context. For example, if the structured binding is declared outside of the class itself, the members must not be private.

Expressive Code With Structured Bindings

If you have a `std::map` of elements, you might know that internally, they are stored as pairs of `<const Key, ValueType>`.

Now, when you iterate through elements of that map:

```cpp
for (const auto& elem : myMap) { /* do stuff */ }
```

You need to write `elem.first` and `elem.second` to refer to the key and value. One of the **coolest use cases** of structured binding is that we can use it inside a range based for loop:

```cpp
std::map<KeyType, ValueType> myMap;
// C++14:
for (const auto& elem : myMap) {
    // elem.first - is the key
    // elem.second - is the value
}


// C++17:
for (const auto& [key,val] : myMap) {
    // use key/value directly
}
```

In the above example, we bind to a pair of `[key, val]` so we can use those names in the loop. Before C++17, you had to operate on an iterator from the map - which returns a pair `<first, second>`. Using real names `key/value` is more expressive.

The above technique can be used in the following example:

Ex 6.4. Iterating through maps with structured binding. Run @Compiler Explorer

```
#include <map>
#include <iostream>

int main() {
    const std::map<std::string, int> mapCityPopulation {
        { "Beijing", 21'707'000 },
        { "London", 8'787'892 },
        { "New York", 8'622'698 }
    };

    for (const auto&[city, population] : mapCityPopulation)
        std::cout << city << ": " << population << '\n';
}
```

In the loop body, you can safely use the `city` and `population` variables.

Initially, structured bindings had some limitations in C++17. For example, you couldn't declare them `static` or `constexpr` or capture them in a lambda. Those issues were removed in C++20 and backported to C++17. The main idea is that a "binding" should behave like a regular variable.

Template Argument Deduction for Class Templates

C++17 filled a gap in the deduction rules for templates. The template argument deduction can occur for class templates and not just for functions.

For instance, to create a `std::pair` object, it was usually more comfortable to write:

```
auto myPair = std::make_pair(42, "hello world"s);
```

Rather than:

```cpp
std::pair<int, std::string> myPair{42, "hello world"};
```

Because `std::make_pair()` is a template function, the compiler can perform the deduction of function template arguments, and there's no need to write:

```cpp
auto myPair = std::make_pair<int, std::string>(42, "hello world");
```

Since C++17, the compiler will nicely deduce the template parameter types for class templates too!

The feature is called *"Class Template Argument Deduction,"* or *CTAD* in short.

In our example, you can now write:

```cpp
std::pair myPair{42, std::string{"hello world"}};
```

CTAD also works with copy initialization and when allocating memory through `new()`:

```cpp
auto otherPair = std::pair{42, "Hello"s};      // also deduced
auto ptr = new std::pair{42, "World"s};         // for new
```

CTAD can substantially reduce complex constructions like:

```cpp
// lock guard:
std::shared_timed_mutex mut;
std::lock_guard<std::shared_timed_mutex> lck(mut);

// array:
std::array<int, 3> arr {1, 2, 3};
```

Can now become:

```cpp
std::shared_timed_mutex mut;
std::lock_guard lck(mut);

std::array arr { 1, 2, 3 };
```

Note that partial deduction cannot happen. You have to specify all the template parameters or none:

```cpp
std::tuple t(1, 2, 3);              // OK: deduction
std::tuple<int,int,int> t(1, 2, 3); // OK: all arguments are provided
std::tuple<int> t(1, 2, 3);         // Error: partial deduction
```

With this feature, many `make_Type` functions might not be needed - especially those that "emulate" template deduction for classes[7].

> CTAD works by using *deduction guides*. Those are "imaginary" functions that are candidates for constructors and their parameters. In many cases, the compiler can use implicitly generated rules, but you can also write your own set of guides. Read more in Class template argument deduction @C++ Reference[8].

Lifetime extension, references, and loops

You might also spot another Modern C++ feature connected to `auto` in the example with the iterating over maps. It's a range-based for loop. The syntax heavily relies on type deduction as it can be used for the type of the element's value during the iteration and to get proper `begin()` and `end()` iterators. In short:

```cpp
for (range-declaration : range-expression) loop-statement
```

As of C++20, it expands into:

```cpp
auto && __range = range-expression;
auto __begin = begin-expr; // usually std::begin()/end() or
auto __end = end-expr;     // something equivalent...
for ( ; __begin != __end; ++__begin) {
    range-declaration = *__begin;
    loop-statement
}
```

As you can see, `range-expression` binds to `__range`, and since it's an rvalue reference, it can support `const` and non `const` ranges. Additionally, since it's an rvalue reference, it can *extend* the lifetime of temporary objects.

We can observe similar behavior for `const` references:

---

[7]Still, there are factory functions that do additional work. For example, `std::make_shared` - it not only creates `shared_ptr`, but also ensures the control block and the pointed object are allocated in one memory region.

[8]https://en.cppreference.com/w/cpp/language/class_template_argument_deduction

```cpp
void fooVec(const std::vector<int>& vec) { }
void fooVecRR(std::vector<int>&& vec) {
    if (!vec.empty())
        vec[0] = 42;
}

fooVec({1, 2, 3});
fooVecRR({1, 2, 3});
```

This time we can pass a temporary vector, created from the initializer list {1, 2, 3}, directly to our two functions. See the code @Compiler Explorer[9].

On the other hand, if you try writing: `void fooVec(vector<int>& vec) { }`, then the compiler will report an error about binding a non-const lvalue reference of type `vector<int>&` to an rvalue of type `std::vector<int>`.

Going back to loops, we also have to consider a more complicated case:

Ex 6.5. Loops and UB in C++20. Run @Compiler Explorer

```cpp
auto getVec() {
    std::vector<std::vector<int>> ints { {1, 2}, {3, 4}, {5, 6} };
    return ints;
}

int main() {
    for (auto& i : getVec()[1])
        std::cout << i;
}
```

This code compiles as of C++20, but it's an Undefined Behaviour! It may crash, print garbage, or even pretend to work fine.

The reason for this situation that we try to bind:

```cpp
auto && __range = getVec()[1];
```

But in the above expression, we have two temporary objects: one big vector from `getVec()` and then its [1] sub "range". C++20 rules only extend the lifetime of [1], and when the expression ends with a semicolon, the big vector ends its lifetime.

---

[9]https://godbolt.org/z/qEKoMe6aj

To have a better solution, you have to store the "big vector" outside:

```
for (auto temp = getVec(); auto& i : temp[1])
    std::cout << i;
```

 This section specifically stressed the C++20 version, as in C++23, a range-based for loop will be much safer with temporary objects! In short, all temporary objects in the `range-expression` part will extend their lifetime. See those accepted proposals: P2644[10] and P2012[11] for more information.

Almost Always Auto

AAA, or Almost Always Auto, is a coding style guideline that recommends using the `auto` keyword for declaring variables in C++. The idea behind this guideline is that using `auto` can make code easier to read and maintain by reducing the amount of boilerplate-type information that needs to be written and maintained.

The core syntax is:

```
auto x = initializer;    // including calling a function
auto y = type{ init };   // forcing a type
```

For example:

```
auto ptr   = std::make_unique<Object>(/*...*/);
auto ptrSh = std::make_shared<Widget>(/*...*/);

std::string computeName(int num) { /* ... */ };
auto str = computeName(42);

auto intro     = std::string { "Hello World" };
auto elapsed   = 42s;         // chrono literals, seconds
auto strElapsed = "42"s;      // std::string literal
```

Ideally, you can also put `const` to indicate that an object won't change:

---

[10] https://wg21.link/P2644
[11] https://wg21.link/P2012

```
const auto str    = computeName(100);
const auto factor = double { 10.1 };
const auto arr    = std::to_array({ 0, 2, 1, 3 });
```

The term was popularlized by Herb Sutter in GotW-94 post[12], GotW 93[13] and GotW 92[14]:

> **Guideline:** Remember that preferring auto variables is motivated primarily by correctness, performance (you're guaranteed that there's no conversion), maintainability, and robustness (If the expression's type is changed, including when a function return type is changed, it just works) and only lastly about typing convenience.

Here are some of the key benefits of using AAA in C++:

- Improved readability: By using `auto`, you can reduce the amount of repetitive type information in your code, making it easier to read and understand.
- Reduced maintenance overhead: With `auto`, you don't need to update the type of a variable when it changes, as the type will be automatically deduced from the initializer. This can save time and reduce the risk of errors.
- Better type safety: The rules for `auto` type deduction in C++ are designed to ensure that the types of variables declared with `auto` are correct and consistent with the initializer. This can help prevent common errors, such as assigning a value of the wrong type to a variable and implicit conversions.
- Ensuring initialization: You cannot leave an `auto` variable not being initialized.

The term uses "almost", so here are the cases when you cannot use this syntax:

---

[12]https://herbsutter.com/2013/08/12/gotw-94-solution-aaa-style-almost-always-auto/
[13]https://herbsutter.com/2013/06/13/gotw-93-solution-auto-variables-part-2/
[14]https://herbsutter.com/2013/06/07/gotw-92-solution-auto-variables-part-1/

```
// when a type consists of two or more names:
auto number = long long { 100 }; // syntax error!
auto num = 100LL;                                // a better alternative

//non-static data member initialization
struct X {
    auto val = int { 10 }; // syntax error
}
```

Additionally, before C++17, you could not initialize things like std::mutex:

```
auto m = std::mutex{};
```

Since mutex is not a moveable type, you couldn't use copy initialization. But this limitation was lifted with C++17's mandatory copy elision.

While the AAA style has some benefits, there are some complaints:

- One potential downside of using automatic style in C++ is that it can make code less readable, especially for developers unfamiliar with the particular style being used. auto x = 42 might be harder to read than just a simple int x = 42.
- Not all developers might be aware of the rules of automatic type deduction, and thus they might introduce some errors or inefficiencies. For example, for (auto x : cont). The code is short, but it will create a copy for each element in a container. The correct form should use auto& x or even auto&& x.
- Similarly assigning auto x = obj.getter_with_reference() might cause an additionally copy when getter_with_reference returns a reference to some internal data. In that case, it's essential to use auto& x.
- When the return type of some function changes in some radical way: for example, from a value type to a reference, it can introduce some unwanted effects in the code that only uses auto val = func().

Summary

This chapter brought several interesting techniques when defining a new variable. Thanks to auto or decltype, you can ask the compiler to infer the type from the expression or an initializer. This might help when a type has a long or complex name (for example, an iterator) or when the type is unknown (like a type of a closure/lambda object). `auto` works similarly to template type deduction. Hence, it removes constness or references from types appearing in the initializer. On the other hand, `decltype` can create an exact type based on other variables and expressions, including their value category. While `auto` and `decltype` were added in C++11, in C++17, we got a nice extension called structured bindings. Bindings can unpack pairs, tuples, arrays, and simple structures, leading to simpler syntax and more expressive code.

In one section, we also looked at AAA, which stands for Almost Always Auto - a convention to declare all variables starting with `auto`. We looked at the benefits of this approach and also some caveats.

At the end of the chapter, I'd like to bring a good quote from the: Google C++ Style guide on type deduction[15]:

> The fundamental rule is: use type deduction only to make the code clearer or safer, and do not use it merely to avoid the inconvenience of writing an explicit type. When judging whether the code is clearer, keep in mind that your readers are not necessarily on your team, or familiar with your project, so types that you and your reviewer experience as unnecessary clutter will very often provide useful information to others. For example, you can assume that the return type of `make_unique<Foo>()` is obvious, but the return type of `MyWidgetFactory()` probably isn't.

---

[15]https://google.github.io/styleguide/cppguide.html#Type_deduction

7. Quiz from Chapters 1...6

Congratulations!

You've just completed the first half of the book! Here's a quick quiz about special member functions and type deduction. Try answering the following questions, and then we will continue our journey :)

You can pick multiple answers in most questions unless explicitly stated otherwise.

1. In a class that doesn't inherit from other types, can you declare a constructor using a different name than the class name?

1. Yes
2. No
3. Yes, but it can be only named self()

2. What operations are called in the following code? Pick one option.

```
std::string s { "Hello World" };
std::string other = s;
```

1. A constructor is called for s. Then, as assignment operation is called for other.
2. A constructor is called for s, and then a copy constructor is called to create other.
3. A constructor is called for s, and then another regular constructor is called for other.

3. Can a constructor return a value using the return statement?

1. Yes, it's like a regular function with a return type of a class name.
2. No, a constructor doesn't have any return type specified.
3. Yes, through a special data member called self_return.

4. Can you mix delegating constructors with data member initialization, like in the constructor `Type(int a, int b)`?

For example:

```
struct Type {
    explicit Type(int a) : a_(a) { }
    explicit Type(int a, int b) : Type(a), b_(b) { }
    int a_;
    int b_;
};
```

1. Yes.
2. Sometimes, depending on if the data members come first.
3. No, the compiler reports an error in this case.

5. Is the following code ok?

```
Product* arr = new Product[10];
// use...
delete arr;
```

Select the true statement:

1. Yes. The code is fine and properly destroys `arr`.
2. This code generates a memory leak as not all elements from `arr` are deleted. The code should use `delete [] arr;`
3. The code uses `delete arr`, which is not necessary as the compiler will properly release all Products.

6. Select true statements

1. Copy initialization considers `explicit` constructors and will use them if there's a matching one.
2. When you pass an argument to a function by value, a copy initialization is used to initialize the function parameter.
3. Aggregate initialization copy-initializes each sub-objects or an array element for which an initializer is provided.

7. What types of y and z variables are declared below?

```
int x = 42;
const auto& y = x;
auto z = y;
```

1. y is const int& and z is int
2. y is int& and z is int&
3. y is const int& and z is int&

8. Which of the following statements are true about structured binding in C++17?

1. Structured binding allows you to bind multiple names to the elements of a tuple.
2. Structured binding allows you to bind multiple names to the fields of a struct.
3. Structured binding allows you to bind multiple names to the elements of an array.

9. What does the following code do?

```
std::vector<int> vec {1, 2, 3, 4, 5};
for (auto elem : vec)
    elem = 10;
```

1. The code doesn't compile, elem cannot be bound to vec.
2. The code compiles. After the loop completes, all vector elements will have a value of 10.
3. The code compiles. After the loop completes, all elements are unchanged.

10. Starting from this line: expr x = 42;. Select true statements:

1. Compiles when expr is int&.
2. Compiles when expr is int.
3. Compiles when expr is const int&.

Please write down your answers and check them in Appendix B.

8. Non-Static Data Member Initialization

You've learned a lot of techniques related to constructors! You can initialize data members in various constructors, delegate them to reuse code, and inherit them from base classes. Yet, we can still improve on assigning default values for data members. I mentioned this feature in the first chapter, where we gave default values for aggregates. We can do the same for classes. And in this chapter, we'll look at the full syntax and options related to this feature.

Please have a look at the example below:

Ex 8.1. NSDMI basics. Run @Compiler Explorer

```cpp
class DataPacket {
    std::string data_;
    size_t checkSum_ { 0 };
    size_t serverId_ { 0 };
public:
    DataPacket() = default;
    DataPacket(const std::string& data, size_t serverId)
    : data_{data}, checkSum_{calcCheckSum(data)}, serverId_{serverId}
    { }
    // getters and setters...
};
```

As you can see, the data members have their default values set at the point of declaration. There's no need to assign default values inside constructors. This feature is much better than a default constructor because it combines declaration and initialization code. This way, it's harder to leave data members uninitialized!

Let's explore this handy feature of Modern C++ in detail.

How it works

This section shows how the compiler "expands" the code to initialize data members.

For a simple declaration:

```
struct SimpleType {
    int field { 0 };
};
```

The code has to behave similarly as you'd define a constructor [1]:

```
struct SimpleType {
    SimpleType() : field(0) { }
    int field;
};
```

Here's the full working example:

Ex 8.2. Basic non-static data member initialization. Run @Compiler Explorer

```
#include <iostream>

struct SimpleType {
    int field { 0 };
};

int main() {
    SimpleType st;
    std::cout << "st.field is " << st.field << '\n';
}
```

As a small exercise, you can experiment with the above sample, assign different values to the `field` data member, and see the changes in the output.

Investigation

With some "machinery," we can see when the compiler performs the initialization.

Let's consider the following type:

---

[1] Technically, those types will be different as the version without the constructor will be considered an aggregate type, but for the purpose of the discussion, it's not essential now.

```cpp
struct SimpleType {
    int a { initA() };
    std::string b { initB() };
    // ...
};
```

The implementations of `initA()` and `initB()` functions have side effects, and they log extra messages:

```cpp
int initA() {
    std::cout << "initA() called\n";
    return 1;
}

std::string initB() {
    std::cout << "initB() called\n";
    return "Hello";
}
```

This allows us to see when the code is called.

Experiments

Now, we can plug in our function and write some additional constructors:

```cpp
struct SimpleType {
    int a { initA() };
    std::string b { initB() };

    SimpleType() { std::cout << "SimpleType()\n"; }
    SimpleType(int x) : a(x) { std::cout << "SimpleType(int)\n"; }
};
```

Here's the test code scenario:

Ex 8.3. Calling **initA** and **initB** functions. Run @Compiler Explorer

```cpp
#include <iostream>
#include <string>

int initA() { /* as above */ }
std::string initB() { /* as above */ }
struct SimpleType { /* as in the snippet above */ };

int main() {
    std::cout << "SimpleType t0\n";
    SimpleType t0;
    std::cout << "SimpleType t1(10)\n";
    SimpleType t1(10);
}
```

After running the code, we can see the following output:

```
SimpleType t0
initA() called
initB() called
SimpleType()
SimpleType t1(10)
initB() called
SimpleType(int)
```

You can observe the following:

t0 is default-initialized; therefore, both fields are initialized with their default values. In other words, the compiler calls {initA()} and {initB{}}. Please notice that they are initialized in the order they appear in the class/struct declaration. Later, the body of the default constructor is called.

In the second case, for t1, only one value is default initialized, and the other comes from the constructor parameter.

As you might already guess, the compiler initializes the fields as if the fields were initialized in a "member initialization list". Therefore, they get the default values before the constructor's body is invoked.

In other words, the compiler "conceptually" expands the code:

```cpp
struct SimpleType {
    int a { initA() };
    std::string b { initB() };
    
    SimpleType() { }
    SimpleType(int x) : a(x) { }
};
```

Into:

```cpp
struct SimpleType {
    int a;
    std::string b;
    
    SimpleType() : a(initA()), b(initB()) { }
    SimpleType(int x) : a(x), b(initB()) { }
};
```

We can also visualize it using the following diagram:

```
data members                                          constructors


int a { initA() };              SimpleType() { }
std::string b { initB() };      SimpleType(int x) : a(x) { }
```

Other forms of NSDMI

Let's try some other examples and see all options that we can initialize a data member using NSDMI:

Ex 8.4. Various syntax for NSDMI. Run @Compiler Explorer

```cpp
struct S {
    int zero {};        // fine, value initialization
    int a = 10;         // fine, copy initialization
    double b { 10.5 };  // fine, direct list initialization
    // short c ( 100 );    // err, direct initialization with parens
    int d { zero + a }; // dependency, risky, but fine
    // double e { *mem * 2.0 }; // undefined!
    int* mem = new int(d); // only for demo, use smart pointers...
    std::unique_ptr<int[]> pInts = std::make_unique<int[]>(10);
    long arr[4] = { 0, 1, 2, 3 };
    std::array<int, 4> moreNumbers { 10, 20, 30, 40};
    // long arr2[] = { 1, 2 }; // cannot deduce
    // auto f = 1;      // err, type deduction doesn't work
    double g { compute() };
    //int& ref { }; // error, cannot set ref to null!
    int& refOk { zero };

    ~S() { delete mem; }
    double compute() { return a*b; }
};
```

Here's the summary:

- zero uses *value* initialization, and thus, it will get the value of 0,
- a uses *copy* initialization,
- b uses direct list initialization,
- c would generate an error as *direct* initialization with parens is not allowed for NSDMI,
- d initializes by reading zero and a, but since d appears later in the list of data members, it's okay, and the order is well-defined,
- e, on the other hand, would have to read from a data member mem, which might not be initialized yet (since it's further in the declaration order), and thus this behavior is undefined,
- mem uses a memory allocation which is also acceptable (but try to stay away from raw new and delete and prefer smart pointers, this code is only for demonstration),
- pInts declares a unique_ptr to an array of 10 integers,

- `arr[4]` declares and initializes an array, but you need to provide the number of elements as the compiler cannot deduce it (as in `arr2`),
- similarly, we can use `std::array<type, count>` for `moreNumbers`, but we need to provide the count and the type of the array elements,
- `f` would also generate an error, as `auto` type deduction won't work,
- `g` calls a member function to compute the value. The code is valid only when that function calls reads from already initialized data members,
- `ref` is commented out because this doesn't compile; you cannot set a null reference,
- on the other hand, `refOk` is potentially acceptable, and does compile, as it's referencing an existing data member.

And here's a simple "demo" to test the S structure:

Ex 8.4. **Various syntax for NSDM - Demo. Run @Compiler Explorer**

```cpp
void showProperties(std::string_view text, const S& s) {
    std::cout << text << '\n';
    std::cout << ".zero: " << s.zero << '\n';
    std::cout << ".a:    " << s.a << '\n';
    std::cout << ".b:    " << s.b << '\n';
    std::cout << ".d:    " << s.d << '\n';
    std::cout << "*.mem: " << *s.mem << '\n';
    std::cout << ".arr[0]: " << s.arr[0] << '\n';
    std::cout << "g:     " << s.g << '\n';
}

int main() {
    S s;       // default initialization
    showProperties("s", s);

    S y { 1 }; // aggregate initialization
    showProperties("y", y);
}
```

The first object s uses default initialization, and it will assign default values to all data members. For the second object, y, I used aggregate initialization with only the first argument, so it will only set the `S::zero` data member.

When we run the code, we can see the following output:

```
s
.zero:    0
.a:       10
.b:       10.5
.d:       10
*.mem:    10
.arr[0]:  0
g:        105
y
.zero:    1
.a:       10
.b:       10.5
.d:       11
*.mem:    11
.arr[0]:  0
g:        105
```

Using the knowledge from this section in our `DataPacket` class, we can be more "creative" and write the following initializers. This version is only an early attempt, not perfect, and we'll improve it later.

Ex 8.5. Dependency in initializers, potentially risky. Run @Compiler Explorer

```
class DataPacket {
    std::string data_ {"empty"};
    size_t checkSum_ { calcCheckSum(data_) };
    size_t serverId_ { 404 };
    /* rest of the code*/
```

Since `checkSum_` is after `data_`, we know the order of initialization, and thus we can safely use `data_` and pass it into `calcCheckSum`.

While the code works and the order of initialization is well defined, such a technique might be problematic to maintain. You might encounter new bugs and complications if you introduce a new data member and reorder class parts. Such an approach might also be harder to read and understand for some people. I mentioned a similar problematic case with a regular initializer list in constructors.

That's why it's best to avoid such dependency and write:

```cpp
inline constexpr auto defaultData {"empty"};
class DataPacket {
    std::string data_ { defaultData };
    size_t checkSum_ { calcCheckSum(defaultData) };
```

Now, it's clear what's the default value, and there's no dependency in the initialization sequence. Here's the corrected version @Compiler Explorer[2]. And we'll look at `inline` variables in a separate chapter.

Copy constructor and NSDMI

The compiler initializes the fields in all the constructors, including the copy and move constructors. However, when a copy or move constructor is the default, there's no need to perform that extra initialization.

Now, let's update our previous examples with copy constructors:

Ex 8.6. Copy constructor and NSDMI. Run @Compiler Explorer

```cpp
#include <iostream>
#include <string>

int initA() {
    std::cout << "initA() called\n";
    return 1;
}

std::string initB() {
    std::cout << "initB() called\n";
    return "World";
}

struct SimpleType {
    int a { initA() };
    std::string b { initB() };

    SimpleType() { }
    explicit SimpleType(std::string s) : b(std::move(s)) { }
```

---

[2]https://godbolt.org/z/9vezbWfbs

```cpp
    SimpleType(const SimpleType& other) {
        std::cout << "copy ctor\n";
        a = other.a;
        b = other.b;
    };
};

int main() {
    SimpleType t1;
    std::cout << "SimpleType t2 = t1:\n";
    SimpleType t2 = t1;
}
```

After running it, we can see the following output:

```
initA() called
initB() called
SimpleType t2 = t1:
initA() called
initB() called
copy ctor
```

The compiler initialized the fields with their default values in the above example. We can see that `initA()` and `initB()` are called just before the `copy ctor` message.

This is why it's better to use the initializer list inside a copy constructor:

```cpp
SimpleType(const SimpleType& other) : a(other.a), b(other.b) {
        std::cout << "copy ctor\n";
    };
```

Now we'll get the following output:

```
SimpleType t1:
initA() called
initB() called
SimpleType t2 = t1:
copy ctor
```

The same happens if you rely on the default copy constructor generated by the compiler (of course, this time, you won't get the output).

```
SimpleType(const SimpleType& other) = default;
```

See the live code @Compiler Explorer[3].

Move constructor and NSDMI

We can observe a similar effect with a move constructor:

Ex 8.7. NSDMI and move constructor. Run @Compiler Explorer

```
#include <iostream>
#include <string>

int initA() {
    std::cout << "initA() called\n";
    return 1;
}

std::string initB() {
    std::cout << "initB() called\n";
    return "World";
}

struct SimpleType {
    int a { initA() };
    std::string b { initB() };
    
    SimpleType() { }
```

---
[3]https://godbolt.org/z/jM8863Wo3

```cpp
    explicit SimpleType(std::string s) : b(std::move(s)) { }

    SimpleType(const SimpleType& other) = default;
    SimpleType(SimpleType&& other) { // only for illustration
        std::cout << "move ctor\n";
        a = std::move(other.a);
        b = std::move(other.b);
    };
};

int main() {
    std::cout << "SimpleType t1:\n";
    SimpleType t1;
    std::cout << "SimpleType t2 = t1:\n";
    SimpleType t2 = std::move(t1);
}
```

When you run the code, you can see that `initA()` and `initB()` are also called only at the start of the move constructor:

```
SimpleType t1:
initA() called
initB() called
SimpleType t2 = t1:
initA() called
initB() called
move ctor
```

This can be fixed by writing a default move constructor:

```cpp
SimpleType(SimpleType&&) = default;
```

or:

```cpp
SimpleType(SimpleType&& other) noexcept
    : a(std::move(other.a)), b(std::move(other.b)) { }
```

You can now experiment with the code example above and see if changing the move constructor reduces the number of invocations of `initA()` and `initB()`.

C++14 changes

Originally, in C++11, if you used default member initialization, your class would lose the "aggregate" status:

```cpp
struct Point { float x = 1.0f; float y = 2.0f; };

// won't compile in C++11
Point myPt { 10.0f, 11.0f };
```

Fortunately, in C++14, the limitation was lifted, and the above line compiles. The aggregate status of the `Point` struct is preserved. You can see and play with the full code below:

Ex 8.8. Aggregates and NSDMI in C++14. Run @Compiler Explorer

```cpp
#include <iostream>

struct Point { float x = 1.0f; float y = 2.0f; };

int main() {
    Point myPt { 10.0f };
    std::cout << myPt.x << ", " << myPt.y << '\n';
}
```

C++20 changes

Since C++11, the code only considered "regular" fields... but how about bit fields in a class? For example:

```cpp
class Type {
    int value : 4;
};
```

Unfortunately, in C++11, it wasn't possible to default-initialize the `value` bit field. However, with a compiler that conforms to C++20, you can write:

Ex 8.9. Bit fields and NSDMI in C++20. Run @Compiler Explorer

```
#include <iostream>

struct Type {
    int value : 4 = 1;
    int second : 4 { 2 };
};

int main() {
    Type t;
    std::cout << t.value << '\n';
    std::cout << t.second << '\n';
}
```

As you can see above, C++20 offers improved syntax where you can specify the default value after the bit size: `var : bit_count { default_value }`.

Limitations of NSDMI

In this section, we'll discuss the current (as of C++20) limitations of non-static data member initialization.

The case with `auto` type deduction

Since we can declare and initialize a variable inside a class, how about using `auto`? It seems natural and follows the AAA (Almost Always Auto) Rule that we've seen in the deduction chapter.

You can use `auto` for static variables:

```
class Type {
    static inline auto theMeaningOfLife = 42; // int deduced
};
```

However, you cannot use it as a class non-static member:

```cpp
class Type {
    auto myField { 0 };     // error
    auto param { 10.5f };   // error
};
```

The alternative syntax also fails:

```cpp
class Type {
    auto myField = int { 10 };
};
```

Unfortunately, `auto` is not supported. For example, in GCC, I get:

```
error: non-static data member declared with placeholder 'auto'
```

It's easy for the compiler to deduce the type of a static data member as the initialization happens at the place you declare it. However, it's not possible for regular data members because the initializer might come from the default member init or the constructor (when you override a default value).

```cpp
class Type {
    auto myField = int { 10 };
};
```
cannot deduce!

The case with Class Template Argument Deduction (CTAD)

As with `auto`, non-static member variables and Class Template Argument Deduction (CTAD) also have limitations.

CTAD has been available since C++17, allowing you to define a class template object without specifying the template arguments. For example:

```
std::pair<double, int> myPair(10.5, 42);
std::vector<float> numbers { 1.1f, 2.2f, 3.3f };
std::array<double, 3> doubles { 1.1, 2.2, 3.3 };
```

In C++17, we can write:

```
std::pair myPair(10.5, 42);
std::vector numbers { 1.1f, 2.2f, 3.3f };
std::array doubles { 1.1, 2.2, 3.3 };
```

The compiler deduces the correct template arguments for `std::pair`, `std::vector`, and `std::array`.

This new functionality works fine for `static` data members of a class:

```
class Type {
    static inline std::vector ints { 1, 2, 3, 4, 5 }; // deduced vector<int>
};
```

However, it does not work as a non-static member:

```
class Type {
    std::vector ints { 1, 2, 3, 4, 5 }; // error!
};
```

On GCC 10.0, I get:

```
error: 'vector' does not name a type
```

Hopefully, both issues presented here are not big blockers, but it's good to be aware of them.

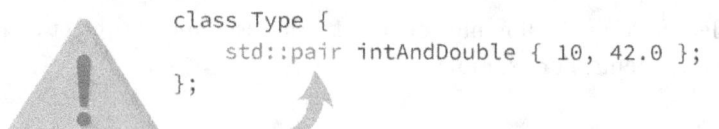

```
class Type {
    std::pair intAndDouble { 10, 42.0 };
};
```
won't deduce template parameters for std::pair

The case with direct initialization and parens[4]

I applied NSDMI to the `DataPacket` class and initialized `data_` to `{"empty"}`.

```cpp
class DataPacket {
    std::string data_ {"empty"};
    // .. the rest...
```

What if I want `data_` to be initialized with 40 stars `*`? I can write the long string or use one of the `std::string` constructors taking a count and a character. Yet, because of a constructor with the `std::initializer_list` in `std::string`, which takes precedence, you need to use direct initialization with parens to call the correct version::

Ex 8.10. Direct initialization with parens and `std::string`. Run @Compiler Explorer

```cpp
#include <iostream>

int main() {
    std::string stars(40, '*');        // parens
    std::string moreStars{40, '*'}; // <<
    std::cout << stars << '\n';
    std::cout << moreStars << '\n';
}
```

If you run the code, you'll see the following:

```
****************************************
(*
```

It's because `{40, '*'}` converts 40 into a character ((using its) ASCI code), and passes those two characters through `std::initializer_list` to create a string with two characters only. The problem is that direct initialization with parens won't work inside a class member declaration:

---

[4]Thanks to Nicolai Josuttis for discussing and clarifying this topic.

```cpp
class DataPacket {
    std::string data_ (40, '*'); // syntax error!
    size_t checkSum_ { calcCheckSum(data_) };
    size_t serverId_ { 404 };
    /* rest of the code*/
```

The code doesn't compile, and to fix this, you can rely on copy initialization:

```cpp
class DataPacket {
    std::string data_ = std::string(40, '*'); // fine
    size_t checkSum_ { calcCheckSum(data_) };
    size_t serverId_ { 404 };
    /* rest of the code*/
```

This limitation is related to the fact that the syntax parens quickly run into the most vexing parse/parsing issues, which is even worse for class members.

There's a separate section on `std::initializer_list` in the book that shares more information about the pros and cons of this helper library type.

How about other constructor types? We'll cover those in the next section.

NSDMI: Advantages and Disadvantages

Let's summarize non-static data member initialization.

Advantages of NSDMI

It looks like using NSDMI is a clear winner for Modern C++. Here are the main reasons why it is so helpful:

- It's easy to write.
- You can be sure that each member is initialized correctly.
- The declaration and the default value are in the same place, so it's easier to maintain.
- It's much easier to conform to the rule that every variable should be initialized.
- It is beneficial when we have several constructors. Previously, we would have to duplicate the initialization code for members or write a custom method, like `InitMembers()`, that would be called in the constructors. Now, you can do a default initialization, and the constructors will only do their specific jobs.

Any negative sides of NSDMI?

On the other hand, the feature has some limitations and inconveniences:

- Using NSDMI makes a class not trivial, as the default constructor (compiler-generated) has to perform some work to initialize data members.
- Performance: When you have performance-critical data structures (for example, a Vector3D class), you may want to have an "empty" initialization code. You risk having uninitialized data members, but you might save several CPU instructions.
- (Only until C++14) NSDMI makes a class non-aggregate in C++11. See the section about C++14 changes.
- They have limitations in the case of `auto` type deduction and CTAD, so you need to provide the type of the data member explicitly.
- You cannot use direct initialization with parens; to fix it, you need list initialization or copy initialization syntax for data members.
- Since the default values are in a header file, any change can require recompiling dependent compilation units. This is not the case if the values are set only in an implementation file.
- Might be hard to read if you rely on calling member functions or depend on other data members.

Summary

Before C++11, the best way to initialize data members was through a member initialization list inside a constructor. Thanks to C++11, we can now initialize data members in the place where we declare them, and the initialization happens just before the constructor body kicks in. Such an approach makes it harder to leave data members in an uninitialized state. In many cases, it also reduces the need to write user-defined constructors that would only set default values.

In the chapter, we covered syntax, how it works with various types of constructors and its limitations. You also saw changes made in C++14 (aggregate classes) and missing bitfield initialization fixed in C++20.

The C++ Core Guidelines advise using NSDMI in at least two sections: C++ Core Guidelines - C.48[5]:

---

[5] https://isocpp.github.io/CppCoreGuidelines/CppCoreGuidelines#c48-prefer-in-class-initializers-to-member-initializers-in-constructors-for-constant-initializers

> **C.48** Prefer in-class initializers to member initializers in constructors for constant initializers:
>
> **Reason**: Makes it explicit that the same value is expected to be used in all constructors. Avoids repetition. Avoids maintenance problems. It leads to the shortest and most efficient code.

And in C++ Core Guidelines - C.45[6]:

> **C.45** Don't define a default constructor that only initializes data members; use in-class member initializers instead.
>
> **Reason**: Using in-class member initializers lets the compiler generate the function for you. The compiler-generated function can be more efficient.

 If you like to read more about NSDMI, I highly recommend reading the book "Embracing Modern C++ Safely", chapter 2, page 318. There's a whole section on advanced cases for this powerful C++ feature.

---

[6]https://isocpp.github.io/CppCoreGuidelines/CppCoreGuidelines#c45-dont-define-a-default-constructor-that-only-initializes-data-members-use-in-class-member-initializers-instead

9. Containers as Data Members

`CarInfo`, `DataPacket`, and `Product` types used relatively simple data members like integers, doubles, or strings. While `std::string` is, in fact, a container (of characters), we tend to use it as an elementary type. In this section, I'd like to discuss more complex data members like arrays, vectors, or maps. First, we'll try to understand the syntax and ways of initializing them, and then you'll learn about `std::initializer_list`.

The basics

If you have a simple structure with various containers, here are some basic ways you can initialize them in a default constructor:

Ex 9.1. The basic syntax for containers as data members. Run @Compiler Explorer

```cpp
struct S {
    S()
    : numbers { 1, 2, 3, 4 }
    // , nums { 1, 2, 3 }
    , doubles { 0.1, 1.1, 2.1 }
    , ints { 100, 101, 102 }
    , moreInts( 10, 1 ) // 10 1's, not 10 and 1
    , names ( 10, "hello" ) // 10 "hello" strings
    , mapping { {"one", 1}, {"two", 2} }
    { }

    int numbers[4];
    // int nums[]; // need to provide the size!
    std::array<double, 3> doubles;
    std::vector<int> ints;
    std::vector<int> moreInts;
    std::vector<std::string> names;
    std::map<std::string, int> mapping;
};
```

```cpp
int main() {
    S s;
    std::cout << "s.numbers[0]: " << s.numbers[0] << '\n';
    std::cout << "s.double[0]: " << s.doubles[0] << '\n';
    std::cout << "s.ints[0]: " << s.ints[0] << '\n';
    std::cout << "s.moreInts[9]: " << s.moreInts[9] << '\n';
    std::cout << "s.names[9]: " << s.names[9] << '\n';
    std::cout << "s.mapping[\"one\"]: " << s.mapping["one"] << '\n';
}
```

Here are the options from the example:

- `int numbers[4];` - is a regular C-style array; we can use aggregate initialization to put the values.
- The syntax with `nums { 1, 2, 3 }`, at line 4, is not an option, as we cannot declare an array without the size and then initialize it later in the initializer list.
- `doubles` is `std::array<double, 3>` which is a C++11-style array, it's also an aggregate type.
- `ints` is a `std::vector` of integers, and we can use list initialization to set elements. Note that there's no need to pass the size/count of those elements.
- `moreInts` is another vector, but this time I used parens () to call the `vector(size_-type count, const T& value = T())` constructor. In this case, braces {} would call the wrong constructor and create a vector with two elements 1 and 10. It's because the value type stored in the container is convertible to the size type (`size_t`). Additionally, according to core guidelines ES.23[1], for constructors with sizes, it's clearer to use parens.
- `names` is a vector of `std::string`, and I also used parens () to call the "size" constructor. This time, the braces {} would also call the "size" constructor as it would be clear to the compiler that {10, "hello"} is not a pair of two elements of the same type.
- `mapping` is `std::map`, and we can also use a handy constructor to pass all pairs of key values at once.

A huge benefit of using standard containers (as regular data members, not pointers) is that there's no need to implement additional special member functions. Copy, move, or the

[1]https://isocpp.github.io/CppCoreGuidelines/CppCoreGuidelines#es23-prefer-the--initializer-syntax

assignment operator works out of the box. Not to mention that there's no need for a custom destructor.

From previous chapters, you know that for default initialization, we can also rely on NSDMI and set the values the moment we declare a data member:

Ex 9.2. Containers as data members and NSDMI. Run @Compiler Explorer

```cpp
struct S {
    int numbers[4] { 1, 2, 3, 4};
    // int nums[] { 0, 1, 2 }; // need to provide the size!
    std::array<double, 3> doubles { 0.1, 1.1, 2.1 };
    std::vector<int> ints { 100, 101, 102};
    std::vector<int> moreInts = std::vector<int>(10, 1);
    std::vector<std::string> names = std::vector<std::string>(10, "hello");
    std::map<std::string, int> mapping { {"one", 1}, {"two", 2} };
};

int main() {
    S s;
    std::cout << "s.numbers[0]: " << s.numbers[0] << '\n';
    std::cout << "s.double[0]: " << s.doubles[0] << '\n';
    std::cout << "s.ints[0]: " << s.ints[0] << '\n';
    std::cout << "s.moreInts[9]: " << s.moreInts[9] << '\n';
    std::cout << "s.names[9]: " << s.names[9] << '\n';
    std::cout << "s.mapping[\"one\"]: " << s.mapping["one"] << '\n';
}
```

In most cases, the NSDMI syntax is convenient and allows us to initialize all container-like members where we declare them. As we discussed in the section on NSDMI and direct initialization, we have to use, for example, a copy initialization to call the vector's constructor using parens (). There's no need to duplicate the code in a constructor, and the S structure can preserve its aggregate status (thus, we can leverage aggregate initialization).

Since C++11, all standard containers can take a list of values into a constructor. For example, before C++11, for std::vector, you'd had to use push_back calls to populate a container with different values. How does the new Standard achieve this? See in the next section.

Using `std::initializer_list`

With the idea of list initialization, there also came support to pass such a list not only to aggregate types. Since C++11, you can use `std::initializer_list<T>`, a lightweight proxy object that provides access to an array of objects of type `const T`.

The Standard shows the following example decl.init.list[2]:

```
struct X {
  X(std::initializer_list<double> v);
};
X x{ 1,2,3 };
```

The initialization will be implemented in a way roughly equivalent to this:

```
const double __a[3] = {double{1}, double{2}, double{3}};
X x(std::initializer_list<double>(__a, __a+3));
```

In other words, the compiler creates a const array and then passes you a proxy object that looks like a regular C++ container with iterators, `begin()`, `end()`, and even the `size()` function. Here's a basic example that illustrates the usage of this type:

Ex 9.3. A function taking **initializer_list**. Run @Compiler Explorer

```
#include <iostream>
#include <initializer_list>

void foo(std::initializer_list<int> list) {
    if (!std::empty(list)) {
        for (const auto& x : list)
            std::cout << x << ", ";
        std::cout << "(" << list.size() << " elements)\n";
    }
    else
        std::cout << "empty list\n";
}
```

---
[2]https://timsong-cpp.github.io/cppwp/n4868/dcl.init.list#5

```cpp
int main() {
    foo({});
    foo({1, 2, 3});
    foo({1, 2, 3, 4, 5});
}
```

In the example, there's a function taking a `std::initializer_list` of integers. Since it looks like a regular container, we can use non-member functions like `std::empty`, use it in a range-based for loop, and check its `size()`. Please notice that there's no need to pass `const initializer_list<int>&` (a const reference) as the initializer list is a lightweight object, so passing by value doesn't copy the referenced elements in the "hidden" array.

Note that we cannot do the same with `std::array` as the parameter to a function would have to have a fixed size. `initializer_list` has a variable length; the compiler takes care of that. Moreover, the "internal" array is created on the stack, so it doesn't require any additional memory allocation (like if you used `std::vector`). The list also takes homogenous values, and the initialization disallows narrowing conversions. For example:

```cpp
// foo({1, 2, 3, 4, 5.5}); // error, narrowing
foo({1, 'x', '0', 10}); // fine, char converted to int
```

There's also a handy use case where you can use range-based for loop directly with the `initializer_list`:

```cpp
#include <iostream>

int main() {
    for (auto x : {"hello", "coding", "world"})
        std::cout << x << ", ";
}
```

The temporary `initializer_list` has an extended lifetime and is visible in the scope of the loop (thanks to binding to an rvalue reference, see the "Lifetime extension" section in the "Type Deduction" chapter). To see the underlying mechanism for this code, you can look at this C++ Insights example[3].

I also have to point out that since `initializer_list` refers to some internal local array, then you should not return it:

---

[3]https://cppinsights.io/s/67363d91

```
std::initializer_list<int> wrong() { // for illustration only!
    return { 1, 2, 3, 4};
}
int main() {
    std::initializer_list<int> x = wrong();
}
```

The above code is equivalent to the following:

```
std::initializer_list<int> wrong() {
    const int arr[] { 1, 2, 3, 4}
    return std::initializer_list<int>{arr, arr+4};
}
int main() {
    std::initializer_list<int> x = wrong();
}
```

The example highlights the error, emphasizing the importance of avoiding similar mistakes in our code. The function returns pointers/iterators to a local object, and that will cause undefined behavior. The compiler should warn about such usage. See a demo @Compiler Explorer[4].

All in all, we can make the following conclusion:

 std::initializer_list is a "view" type; it references some implementation-dependent and a local array of const values. Use it mainly for passing into functions when you need a variable number of arguments of the same type. If you try to return such lists and pass them around, then you risk lifetime issues. Use with care.

Constructors taking std::initializer_list

As mentioned, all containers from the Standard Library have constructors supporting initializer_list. For instance:

---

[4]https://godbolt.org/z/bonveWf4a

```cpp
// the vector class:
constexpr vector( std::initializer_list<T> init,
                  const Allocator& alloc = Allocator() );
// map:
map( std::initializer_list<value_type> init,
     const Compare& comp = Compare(),
     const Allocator& alloc = Allocator() );
```

How does it work? Let's see a class with a user-declared constructor taking the list:

Ex 9.4. A test constructor with `initializer_list`. Run @Compiler Explorer

```cpp
#include <iostream>
#include <initializer_list>

struct X {
    X(std::initializer_list<int> list)
     : count{list.size()} { puts("X(init_list)"); }
    X(size_t cnt) : count{cnt} { puts("X(cnt)"); }
    X() { puts("X()"); }
    size_t count {};
};

int main() {
    X x;
    std::cout << "x.count = " << x.count << '\n';
    X y { 1 };
    std::cout << "y.count = " << y.count << '\n';
    X z { 1, 2, 3, 4 };
    std::cout << "z.count = " << z.count << '\n';
    X w ( 3 );
    std::cout << "w.count = " << w.count << '\n';
}
```

The X class defines three constructors, and one of them takes `initializer_list`. If we run the program, you'll see the following output:

```
X()
x.count = 0
X(init_list)
y.count = 1
X(init_list)
z.count = 4
X(cnt)
w.count = 3
```

As you can see, writing `X x;` invokes a default constructor. Similarly, if you write `X x{};`, the compiler won't call a constructor with the empty initializer list. But in other cases, the list constructor is "greedy" and will take precedence over the regular constructor taking one argument. To call the exact constructor, you need to use direct initialization with parens ().

Example implementation

Let's go further with containers and have some more realistic examples. I want to show you the `Package` class that holds several `Product` objects. As an additional complexity, inside this `Package` class, let's count the total value of the package, as well as count products by name. Here's the `Product` class (similar to our previous declarations):

```cpp
struct Product {
    Product() = default;
    Product(std::string s, double v)
    : name{std::move(s)}, value{v} { }

    std::string name;
    double value{};
};
```

And the `Package` class:

```cpp
class Package {
public:
    void addProduct(const Product& p) {
        ++counts_[p.name];
        prods_.push_back(p);
        totalValue_ += p.value;
    }
    void printContents() const {
        for (auto& [key, val] : counts_)
            std::cout << key << ", count: " << val<< '\n';
        std::cout << "total value: " << totalValue_ << '\n';
    }
private:
    std::vector<Product> prods_; // all products
    std::map<std::string, unsigned> counts_;
    double totalValue_ { };
};
```

The Package class holds all objects that we pass through the AddProduct() member function and also performs some internal changes: it counts the total sum of values and also adds the product to the counts_ dictionary. We can run this code with the following client code:

Ex 9.5. The Package class demo. Run @Compiler Explorer

```cpp
struct Product { /*as before*/ };
class Package { /*as above*/ };

int main() {
    Package pack;
    pack.addProduct({"crayons", 3.0});
    pack.addProduct({"pen", 2.0});
    pack.addProduct({"bricks", 11.0});
    pack.addProduct({"bricks", 12.0});
    pack.addProduct({"pen", 12.0});
    pack.addProduct({"pencil", 12.0});
    pack.printContents();
}
```

And not surprisingly, we'll get the following output:

```
bricks, count: 2
crayons, count: 1
pen, count: 2
pencil, count: 1
total value: 52
```

While the code looks correct, this approach has at least one inconvenience. The client must use addProduct several times to populate the internal containers. This can be improved by creating a constructor (as well as some function overloads) that would take whole containers:

```
Package(const std::vector<Product>& items) {
    for (const auto& elem : items)
        addProduct(elem);
}
```

Having a function taking more elements at once might be handy if you process a bulk of data. For example, loading products from a file or getting a network packet.

On the other hand, for unit tests or test code, you might want to initialize your objects with a list of objects. In the case of taking std::vector you have to write.

```
Package pack {
    std::vector<Product>{{"pen", 1.0}, {"pencil", 2.0}}
};
```

Notice the additional pair of braces. The first pair opens a call to a constructor, and the next creates a temporary vector which is later passed to the constructor. On the other hand, you can also use std::initializer_list and get a simpler syntax:

Ex 9.6. The Package class with `initializer_list`. Run @Compiler Explorer

```cpp
struct Product { /*as before*/ };

class Package {
public:
    Package() = default;
    Package(std::initializer_list<Product> items) {
        for (auto& elem : items)
            addProduct(elem);
    }

    void addProduct(const Product& p) {
        ++counts_[p.name];
        prods_.push_back(p);
        totalValue_ += p.value;
    }
    void printContents() const {
        for (auto& [key, val] : counts_)
            std::cout << key << ", count: " << val<< '\n';
        std::cout << "total value: " << totalValue_ << '\n';
    }
private:
    std::vector<Product> prods_; // all products
    std::map<std::string, unsigned> counts_;
    double totalValue_ { };
};

int main() {
    Package pack {
        {"pen", 1.0}, {"pencil", 2.0}
    };
    pack.addProduct({"crayons", 3.0});
    pack.addProduct({"pen", 2.0});
    pack.addProduct({"bricks", 11.0});
    pack.addProduct({"bricks", 12.0});
    pack.printContents();
}
```

In the example above, there are two constructors: one default and another with `std::initializer_list`. I had to specify a default constructor, so it's possible to create `Package emptyPackage;`, as `initializer_list` doesn't allow us to pass empty lists `{}` or use default initialization.

What's an advantage over passing `std::vector`? Apart from nested braces, `std::vector` requires a dynamic allocation for a memory block to store its elements. For `std::initializer_list` the compiler deduces the size and creates a C-style array underneath for elements, so there's no extra allocation here.

We're also not limited to only constructors, as we can use `initializer_list` in regular functions:

```
Package(std::initializer_list<Product> items) {
    addProducts(items);
}

void addProduct(const Product& p) { /* as before */ }

void addProducts(std::initializer_list<Product> items) {
    for (auto& elem : items)
        addProduct(elem);
}
```

The example above shows just a part of implementing the `Package` class. I created a new member function, `addProducts`, which takes `initializer_list` and calls `addProduct` to perform the main job. The constructor is also updated to call the new function and doesn't duplicate code.

The cost of copying elements

Passing elements through `std::initializer_list` is very convenient, but it's good to know that when you pass it to a `std::vector`'s constructor (or other standard containers), each element has to be copied. It's because, conceptually, objects in the `initializer_list` are put into a `const` temporary array, so they have to be copied to the container. See the following example which compares `push_back` with `emplace_back` and `initializer_list`:

Ex 9.7. Extra copy in `initializer_list`. Run @Compiler Explorer

```cpp
struct Value {
    Value(int x) : v(x) { cout << "Value(" << v << ")\n"; }
    Value(const Value& rhs) : v{rhs.v} { cout << "copy Value(" << v << ")\n"; }
    Value(Value&& rhs) : v{rhs.v}  {cout << "move Value(" << v << ")\n"; }
    ~Value() noexcept { cout << "~Value(" << v << ")\n"; }
    int v {0};
};

int main() {
    std::vector<Value> vals { 1, 2 };
    std::vector<Value> moreVals;
    moreVals.reserve(4);
    std::cout << "with emplace... \n";
    moreVals.emplace_back(3);
    moreVals.emplace_back(4);
    std::cout << "with push... \n";
    moreVals.push_back(5);
    moreVals.push_back(6);
}
```

If we run the program, we'll get the following output:

```
Value(1)
Value(2)
copy Value(1)
copy Value(2)
~Value(2)
~Value(1)
with emplace...
Value(3)
Value(4)
with push...
Value(5)
move Value(5)
~Value(5)
Value(6)
move Value(6)
```

~Value(6)
... other destructors ...

As you can see, in the case of `initializer_list`, we have two constructors called and then two copy constructors. Then two destructors for those temporary objects are called. In the case of `emplace_back()`, the compiler creates objects "in place", so there's no need to copy or even move objects around. In the case of `push_back()`, the temporary object is created, which can then be "moved" to the final destination.

Similarly, when you initialize `std::vector` of `std::string` with `initializer_list`, you will get extra copies:

```
std::vector<std::string> words { "Hello", "World" };
```

In the above case, two temporary string objects are created from string literals and then copied into the container.

Some inconvenience - non-copyable types

In the previous section, we spoke about extra copy that we'd get with the `initializer_list`, which also causes issues when your objects are not copyable. For example, when you want to create a vector of `unique_ptr`.

Ex 9.8. Trying to pass **unique_ptr**. Run @Compiler Explorer

```cpp
#include <vector>
#include <memory>

struct Shape {    virtual void render() const ; };
struct Circle : Shape { void render() const override; };
struct Rectangle : Shape { void render() const override; };

int main() {
    std::vector<std::unique_ptr<Shape>> shapes {
        std::make_unique<Circle>(), std::make_unique<Rectangle>()
    };
}
```

The line where I want to create a vector fails to compile, and we get many messages about copying issues. The unique pointers cannot be copied, they can only be moved, and passing `initializer_list` doesn't give us any options to handle those cases. The only way to build such a container is to use `emplace_back` or `push_back`:

```
std::vector<std::unique_ptr<Shape>> shapes;
shapes.reserve(2);
shapes.push_back(std::make_unique<Circle>());            // or
shapes.emplace_back(std::make_unique<Rectangle>());
```

See the working code at Compiler Explorer[5].

More options (advanced)

Is `std::initializer_list` the best way to pass a list of homogenous values? It has some uses and might be good enough for classes that look like containers, and you want to provide a handy way of passing a list of values at once. But, we can also leverage some template techniques and use variadic function templates.

Ex 9.9. A variadic function template. Run @Compiler Explorer

```
template<typename... Ts>
requires (std::same_as<Ts, Product> && ...)
void addProducts(const Product & first, const Ts&... args) {
    addProduct(first);
    (addProduct(args), ...);
}
pack.addProducts({"pencil", 12.0}, Product{"pen", 10});
//pack.addProducts({"pencil", 12.0}, 10); // error, 10 is not a Product
```

I don't want to go into full details, as it's outside the scope of the book, but here are the core features that enable such code:

- Variadic templates allow us to pass any number of arguments into a function and process it with argument pack syntax.

---
[5]https://godbolt.org/z/E7h4vzYP4

- Concepts from C++20 add a way to require all input types to be `Product`. For example, in the last line, I tried to pass `10` as the second argument to the function, and the compiler generated an error that the integer `10` didn't match the concept requirements.
- `(addProduct(args), ...);` is a fold expression over a comma operator that nicely expands the argument pack at compile time. Fold expressions have been available since C++17.
- The code might also be updated with rvalue references (forming a universal reference) which would be forwarded to the internal function.

We can similarly write a function for `unique_ptr`:

Ex 9.10. Initialization from a list of unique pointers. Run @Compiler Explorer

```cpp
template<typename T, typename... Args>
auto initFromMoveable(Args&&... args) {
    std::vector<std::unique_ptr<T>> vec;
    vec.reserve(sizeof...(Args));
    (vec.emplace_back(std::forward<Args>(args)), ...);
    return vec;
}
int main() {
    auto shapes = initFromMoveable<Shape>(
        std::make_unique<Circle>(),
        std::make_unique<Rectangle>()
    );
}
```

For more information about those techniques, have a look at articles at the C++Stories blog: C++20 Concepts - a Quick Introduction[6], C++ Templates: How to iterate through std::tuple: the Basics[7].

> `std::initializer_list` has a bad reputation in C++. You can see this in Jason Turner's talk from C++Now 2018, "Initializer Lists are Broken — Let's Fix Them."[8] and understand different solutions to passing lists to a function. And look at this article by Andrzej Krzemieński about The cost of `std::initializer_list`[9].

---

[6]https://www.cppstories.com/2021/concepts-intro/
[7]https://www.cppstories.com/2022/tuple-iteration-basics/
[8]https://www.youtube.com/watch?v=sSlmmZMFsXQ
[9]https://akrzemi1.wordpress.com/2016/07/07/the-cost-of-stdinitializer_list/

Summary

In this chapter, we discussed having various containers as data members. If we use containers from the Standard Library, then they handle all memory management and allocations. We can use those standard containers as regular types without worrying about custom implementation for special member functions. Thanks to the NSDMI feature, we can safely initialize them with a convenient syntax. In the second part of the chapter, you learned about `initializer_list`, which is an option to pass multiple values at once with a handy API. The `initializer_list` type is only a view of an internal array of `const` objects. For simple types, `initializer_list` has some benefits, but you must be aware of the extra copy when passing things around. Additionally, if you have a constructor taking the list, then it will be "greedy" and takes priority over other non-default constructors.

10. Non-regular Data Members

Thus far, we have spoken about mutable non-static data members like integers, doubles, or strings. Such objects are regular[1], meaning they are copyable, default constructible, and equally comparable.

However, you can also have other categories of objects in a class. For example, a custom type might contain constant data members, pointers, references, or moveable-only fields like unique pointers or mutexes. For such members, the compiler will have issues creating default implementations for special member functions.

In this chapter, we'll shed some light on such cases.

Constant non-static data members

Consider the following code with a `const` data member `id_`:

Ex 10.1. A constant data member. Run @Compiler Explorer

```
#include <iostream>
#include <string>

class ProductConst {
public:
    explicit ProductConst(const char* name, unsigned id)
    : name_(name), id_(id) { }

    const std::string& name() const { return name_; }
    void name(const std::string& name) { name_ = name; }
    unsigned id() const { return id_; }
private:
    std::string name_;
    const unsigned id_;
};
```

---

[1]Being regular is a well-defined term in the C++ Standard, see the `std::regular` concept at C++ Reference: https://en.cppreference.com/w/cpp/concepts/regular.

```cpp
int main() {
    ProductConst tvset{"TV Set", 123};
    std::cout << tvset.name() << ", id: " << tvset.id() << '\n';
    ProductConst copy { tvset };
    std::cout << copy.name() << ", id: " << copy.id() << '\n';
}
```

In the example above, the class `ProductConst` has a constant data member `id_`. We can set the constant inside the constructor; from now on, it will be fixed, and we won't be able to change its value.

At first sight, the code looks fine, and we can even use the default copy constructor to create copy from tvset. But, we have a few issues:

First of all, the default constructor is blocked:

```cpp
class ProdConst {
public:
    ProdConst() = default; // warning in clang!
```

In Clang, you'll get the following warning:

```
default constructor of 'ProdConst' is implicitly deleted because field
'id_' of const-qualified type 'const unsigned int' would not be initialized
```

You can attempt to fix it with in-class member initialization:

```cpp
private:
    std::string name_;
    const unsigned id_ { 0 };
};
```

However, this is semantically confusing as you won't be able to change that member later.
You might also be surprised when you try to change the value of tvset:

```
tvset = Product("TV Set 2022", 456);
```

The line generates a compilation error! It's because the compiler tries to invoke an assignment operator, but it's impossible since one data member is constant. When one data member is `const`, the compiler won't generate a default assignment operator for us. Such classes might also cause trouble in standard containers. Consider the following code:

```
std::vector<ProdConst> prods;
prods.push_back(ProdConst("box", 234));
prods.push_back(ProdConst("car", 567));
prods.insert(prods.begin(), ProductConst("ball", 987));
```

While the `push_back` calls work fine (as the compiler can successfully create objects inside the container), there's an issue with the `insert()`, which requires an assignment operator to be available.

GCC might report the following error:

```
error: use of deleted function ProdConst& ProdConst::operator=(ProdConst&&)
```

You can experiment with this example @Compiler Explorer[2].

The only way to fix the compiler error is to write a custom assignment operator. For example, you could copy mutable data members and "leave" constant members. The problem is that it's pretty complicated. Moreover, it might be misleading to the reader, as it's not easy to reason what is changing.

If you want your object to be constant, make it `const` as a "whole" rather than just some of its parts.

You can read more about this semantic problem with constant data members in a good overview by Arthur O'Dwyer; see at `const` all the things?[3].

We can summarize a class type with a `const` non-static data member as:
- It will be default constructible only when you assign a default value to the member (NSDMI); otherwise, it won't be default constructible.
- The compiler can generate a copy and move constructors.
- Default copy assignment and move assignment operators are blocked.

---
[2]https://godbolt.org/z/oeazxj5qs
[3]https://quuxplusone.github.io/blog/2022/01/23/dont-const-all-the-things/

Pointers as data members

This section should start with a warning: "don't use raw pointers", but if you do, please be careful. Have a look at the following dangerous wrapper:

Ex 10.2. A raw pointer as a data member. Run @Compiler Explorer

```cpp
#include <iostream>
#include <string>

class DangerousWrapper {
public:
    explicit DangerousWrapper(std::string* pstr) : pName_(pstr) { }

    std::string* name() const { return pName_; }
    void name(std::string* pstr) { pName_ = pstr; }
private:
    std::string* pName_ { nullptr };
};

int main() {
    std::string str { "Name"};
    DangerousWrapper w { &str };
    DangerousWrapper x { w };
    std::cout << *w.name() << '\n'; // urgh... !!
    *(x.name()) = "Other";
    std::cout << *w.name() << '\n'; // urgh... !!
}
```

It looks simple. `pName_` is a raw pointer to `std::string`, and when used correctly, it seems to work. A pointer can be copied and assigned; thus, the compiler creates the default copy constructor, move constructor, copy assignment and move assignment.

But the main point and risk are that it's tricky to use such wrappers!

Every time you access a pointer, you should check if it's not null. For example, this line:

```cpp
*(w.name())
```

It can generate undefined behavior if `pName_` is null. In practical terms, you'll probably get a runtime crash on x86/64 platforms like Windows or Linux.

What's more, you have to be prepared for cases like:

```cpp
DangerousWrapper foo() {
    std::string str { "Name"};
    DangerousWrapper w { &str };
    // some computation...
    return w;
}
auto x = foo(); // oops... !!
```

What might happen here?

The code returns a wrapper that holds a pointer to a local object. After the function ends, the local `str` variable goes out of the scope, and `pName_` will point to some garbage. In that case, checking for `!= nullptr'` won't help.

Our simple wrapper might be considered as a `view` type of object. Such types rely on the existence of some other objects declared in the same or a different scope. In the Standard Library, we can mention at least two similar types:

- `std::string_view` (from C++17)
- `std::span` (from C++20)

However, we can also use pointers internally in a class and don't take or expose them directly. One of the best examples is a pointer to implementation, called `pimpl` as a popular abbreviation[4].

Here's one version of the pattern and raw pointers:

---

[4]PIMPL is often used to reduce compilation times, and in C++20, this might not be needed because of modules. Still, PIMPL can be handy when you want to hide the implementation details and protect against ABI changes completely.

```
// class.h
class MyClassImpl;
class MyClass {
    // special member functions...
    void Foo();
private:
    MyClassImpl* pImpl_ {};
};

// class.cpp
class MyClassImpl {
public:
    void DoStuff() { /*...*/ }
};

MyClass::MyClass () : pImpl_(new MyClassImpl()) { }
MyClass::~MyClass () { delete pImpl_; }

void MyClass ::DoSth() {
    m_pImpl->DoSth();
}
```

In short, we declare a pointer to some incomplete type in the header file. A pointer has a well-defined size (usually 4 or 8 bytes), so the compiler can adequately evaluate the size of the `MyClass` class, even though it points to some incomplete `MyClassImpl`. Inside the cpp file, we declare and define the implementation class. The main class becomes a thin wrapper that calls the implementation through that `pImpl_` pointer. The main thing to notice here is that the lifetime of the pointer is strictly related to the lifetime of the parent class. If you create `MyClass`, you also start the lifetime of `pImpl_`. The pointer to implementation is not exposed outside, the clients of the class cannot change it directly, so it's safe to use.

While the compiler can create default copy and move operations, those will produce only "shallow" copies since the pointer will be copied bit by bit. We must implement special member functions to allocate new pointers for implementation objects properly.

You can read about all benefits of this pattern in my article The Pimpl Pattern - what you should know - C++ Stories[5].

Pointer to implementation is one of many examples where a pointer might be handy. We

---

[5]https://www.cppstories.com/2018/01/pimpl/

can also list a few ideas:

- Having a pointer to some cache. The cache might be created on demand and updated when needed.
- Having a pointer to some large buffers that won't fit into the stack[6].
- If the class requires some pointers for C-style libraries, like file handlers, sockets, OS objects, etc.

In all of the above cases, the lifetime of the stored pointer is "inside" or wrapped by the lifetime of the parent class/object. It's tricky but usually safer than when you rely on entities totally "outside" the object.

 Raw pointers are usually tricky to use, so be careful or use smart pointers.

In summary, a class type with a raw pointer non-static data member has the following properties:

- It will be default constructible, but it's best to assign some starting value to the pointer (or at least `nullptr`).
- The compiler can generate a copy and move constructors, but it will be a shallow copy!
- The compiler can create default copy assignment and move assignment operators, but the operations will also be shallow!

Smart pointers as data members

If you need to use a pointer as a data member, consider using a smart pointer. The main benefit of smart pointers is that they wrap resource creation and deletion. That's why you don't need to remember about releasing a resource manually. Let's have a look at the example which shows a `unique_ptr` inside a class:

---

[6]If the buffer is global or `static`, then non-stack memory is used, and the stack size limitation doesn't apply. Thanks to JFT for the note!

Ex 10.3. A unique pointer as a data member. Run @Compiler Explorer

```cpp
struct Value {
    explicit Value(int v) : v_(v) { std::cout << "Value(" << v_ << ")\n"; }
    ~Value() noexcept { std::cout << "~Value(" << v_ << ")\n"; }
    int v_;
};

class ProductUniquePointer {
public:
    ProductUniquePointer() = default;
    explicit ProductUniquePointer(const char* name,
                                  std::unique_ptr<Value> pId)
    : name_(name), pId_(std::move(pId)) { }

    const std::string& name() const { return name_; }
    int id() const { return pId_ ? pId_->v_ : 0; }
private:
    std::string name_;
    std::unique_ptr<Value> pId_;
};
```

This time the code is a bit more complex, but the main benefit is that we increase the safety of the code. The code uses a simple `Value` wrapper type which can output some text from the constructor and the destructor.

For example, here's a simple use case:

```cpp
auto pId = std::make_unique<Value>(123);
ProductUniquePointer tvset{"TV Set", std::move(pId)};
std::cout << "tvset: " << tvset.name() << ", id: " << tvset.id() << '\n';
ProductUniquePointer moved { std::move(tvset) };
std::cout << "tvset: " << tvset.name() << ", id: " << tvset.id() << '\n';
std::cout << "moved: " << moved.name() << ", id: " << moved.id() << '\n';
```

The code creates `pId` and then passes it to the `tvset` object. Notice that we have to explicitly "move" it. This transfers the ownership of the resource (allocated memory for the `Value` object) into the `ProductUniquePointer` instance. At each moment, there's only one ("unique") owner of the resource. Later, we move the whole object to create `moved`. Here's the output from this program:

```
Value(123)
tvset: TV Set, id: 123
tvset: , id: 0
moved:  TV Set, id: 123
~Value(123)
```

Notice that the `Value` destructor is called automatically and only once. And after we move from `tvset`, the default move constructor is called, and the `tvset` object is left in an unspecified but valid state (usually an "empty" state).

Since the class doesn't implement any special member functions, the compiler will provide the default implementations. In the case of a `unique_ptr` data member, copy operations are blocked, but move operations are provided. This limitation is a good thing, as we have to decide on the semantics of the class and implement custom copy operations.

Safer wrappers with `unique_ptr`

`unique_ptr` can also help with objects going out of the scope we've seen with `DangerousWrapper`. Below you have a version with a replaced raw pointer with a smart pointer; the code won't compile:

```cpp
#include <string>
#include <memory>

class SaferWrapper {
public:
    explicit SaferWrapper(unique_ptr<string> pstr)
    : pName_(move(pstr)) { }

    string* name() const { return pName_.get(); }
    void name(unique_ptr<string> pstr) { pName_ = move(pstr); }
private:
    unique_ptr<string> pName_ {nullptr};
};

SaferWrapper foo() {
    string str { "Name" };
    SaferWrapper w { &str };
    // some computation...
```

```
    return w;
}

int main() { }
```

The `SaferWrapper` takes a `unique_ptr` as an argument for the constructor. This will immediately block the passing of a raw pointer `&str`, and GCC reports the following error:

```
error: no matching function for call to 'SaferWrapper::SaferWrapper(...)'
   20 |          SaferWrapper w { &str };
```

To fix the issue, we can write:

```
// 1)
std::string str { "Name"};
SaferWrapper w { std::make_unique<std::string>(str) };
// 2):
SaferWrapper w { std::make_unique<std::string>("Name") };
```

Above the first case, 1) creates a temporary unique pointer with a **copy** of the `str` object. In the second case, there's no extra string copy, and the pointer is created from the `"Name"` string literal. In both cases, the string object is allocated on the heap, so even if the function ends, the pointer will still be valid.

Of course, you can still write the following code:

```
// bad idea:
std::string str { "Name"};
SaferWrapper w { std::unique_ptr<std::string>(&str) };
```

But in this case, the unique pointer will still point to some local object, and when it goes out of scope, it will be invalid. As you can see, `unique_ptr` gives us a safer technique, but still, you need to pay attention when you create it.

Improving `pimpl` with `unique_ptr`

Going further, here's an improved version, which uses `unique_ptr` based on our previous code. This class "wraps" the pointer, and the code implements all special member functions to manage it properly.

Ex 10.4. PIMPL with `unique_ptr`, header. Run @Wandbox

```cpp
// class.h
#include <memory>

class MyClassImpl;
class MyClass {
public:
    MyClass();
    ~MyClass();
    // movable:
    MyClass(MyClass && rhs) noexcept;
    MyClass& operator=(MyClass && rhs) noexcept;
    // and copyable
    MyClass(const MyClass& rhs);
    MyClass& operator=(const MyClass& rhs);

    void DoSth();
    void DoConst() const;
private:
    const MyClassImpl* Pimpl() const { return m_pImpl.get(); }
    MyClassImpl* Pimpl() { return m_pImpl.get(); }

    std::unique_ptr<MyClassImpl> m_pImpl;
};
```

And the source file:

Ex 10.4. PIMPL with `unique_ptr`, cpp file. Run @Wandbox

```cpp
// class.cpp
#include "class.h"
#include <iostream>

class MyClassImpl {
public:
    ~MyClassImpl() = default;
    void DoSth() { std::cout << "Impl::DoSth()\n"; }
    void DoConst() const { }
};
```

```cpp
MyClass::MyClass() : m_pImpl(std::make_unique<MyClassImpl>()) { }

MyClass::~MyClass() = default;
MyClass::MyClass(MyClass &&) noexcept = default;
MyClass& MyClass::operator=(MyClass &&) noexcept = default;

MyClass::MyClass(const MyClass& rhs)
    : m_pImpl(std::make_unique<MyClassImpl>(*rhs.m_pImpl)) { }

MyClass& MyClass::operator=(const MyClass& rhs) {
    if (this != &rhs)
        m_pImpl = std::make_unique<MyClassImpl>(*rhs.m_pImpl);

    return *this;
}

void MyClass::DoSth() {
    std::cout << "MyClass::DoSth() wrapper\n";
    Pimpl()->DoSth();
}

void MyClass::DoConst() const {
    Pimpl()->DoConst();
}
```

The above code uses `unique_ptr` to hold the pointer to "implementation". The class defines special member functions so that when you copy an object, you'll copy the implementation details.

Using `std::shared_ptr`

On the other hand, we can also use `shared_ptr`, which has different semantics. Rather than restricting the resource to a single owner, `shared_ptr` works with several owners that share a single resource. When the last owner ends its lifetime, the resource is also deleted. Here's a simplified demo of such behavior:

Ex 10.5. A shared pointer as a data member. Run @Compiler Explorer

```cpp
struct Value {
    explicit Value(int v) : v_(v) { cout << "Value(" << v_ << ")\n"; }
    ~Value() noexcept { cout << "~Value(" << v_ << ")\n"; }
    int v_;
};

class ProductWithSharedPtr {
public:
    ProductWithSharedPtr() = default;
    explicit ProductWithSharedPtr(const char* name,
                                  std::shared_ptr<Value> pId)
    : name_(name), pId_(pId) { }

    const std::string& name() const { return name_; }
    int id() const { return pId_ ? pId_->v_ : 0; }
private:
    std::string name_;
    std::shared_ptr<Value> pId_;
};
```

We can use it like:

```cpp
int main() {
    auto pId = make_shared<Value>(123);
    ProductWithSharedPtr tv{"TV Set", pId};
    cout << "tv: " << tv.name() << ", id: " << tv.id() << '\n';
    cout << "pId use count: " << pId.use_count() << '\n';
    {
        ProductWithSharedPtr copy { tv };
        cout << "tv: " << tv.name() << ", id: " << tv.id() << '\n';
        cout << "copy: " << copy.name() << ", id: " << copy.id() << '\n';
        pId->v_ = 100;
        cout << "tv: " << tv.name() << ", id: " << tv.id() << '\n';
        cout << "copy: " << copy.name() << ", id: " << copy.id() << '\n';
        cout << "pId use count: " << pId.use_count() << '\n';
    }
```

```
        cout << "pId use count: " << pId.use_count() << '\n';
}
```

```
Value(123)
tv: TV Set, id: 123
pId use count: 2
tv: TV Set, id: 123
copy:  TV Set, id: 123
tv: TV Set, id: 100
copy:  TV Set, id: 100
pId use count: 3
pId use count: 2
~Value(100)
```

As you can see, we still have a single `Value` resource, and then we pass it to the `tvset` object. When we copy the object into `copy`, the pointer is shared (the resource is not copied). This is safer than a shallow copy of a raw pointer because we have precise semantics, and we can see where are the owners of the resource. For example, when `copy` goes out of scope, it won't `delete` the `Value` object; it will just decrease the reference counter (see "use count" going from 3 to 2). In the end, `tvset` as well as `pId` goes out of scope, the reference counter decreases to zero, and thus the memory block is deleted.

Summary for smart pointers

In summary, a class type with a smart pointer non-static data member has the following properties:

- It will be default constructible, but it's best to assign some starting value to the pointer (or at least `nullptr`).
- The compiler can generate a move constructor and move assignment operator.
- For `unique_ptr` default copy operations are blocked, and you must implement custom versions.
- For `shared_ptr`, default copy operations are provided, but they are "shallow". This is still safer than copying raw pointers, as this time, we copy shared pointers which increases their internal reference counter, and thus the resource handling will be safe (although it might be harder to reason about).

References as data members

We covered `const` and pointers, and now we can finally address references as data members. But before, we need to recall `const` pointers:

```
// value being pointed cannot be changed:
const int* pInt;
int const* pInt; // equivalent form

// address of the pointer cannot be changed,
// but the value being pointed can be
int* const pInt;

// both value and the address of the pointer are protected from changing
const int* const pInt;
int const* const pInt; // equivalent form
```

And in most cases, we can look at references, like the `T* const ptr` type. In other words, we can initialize the reference with some other object, but we cannot rebind it later. This immediately brings consequences as we had with `const` data members:

- Default constructor is problematic, as we cannot assign `nullptr` to a reference.
- Default copy and move constructors are provided by the compiler, but they are "shallow", like with a pointer.
- Default copy and move assignment operators are deleted, as the compiler cannot implement them for a const data member.

See the example:

```cpp
#include <iostream>

class WrapperWithRef {
public:
    WrapperWithRef() = default; // cannot make it default...
    explicit WrapperWithRef(std::string& n) : name_(n) { }

    const std::string& name() const { return name_; }
    void name(const std::string& name) { name_ = name; }
private:
    std::string& name_; // cannot set to "nullptr" or {} empty!
};

int main() {
    std::string str { "Name"};
    WrapperWithRef w { str };
    w.name(str);
    WrapperWithRef x { w };
    std::cout << "str:       " << str << '\n';
    std::cout << "x.name(): " << x.name() << '\n';
    x.name("abc");
    std::cout << "str:       " << str << '\n';

    //WrapperWithRef def {}; // cannot default construct
    //x = w; // error, cannot assign
}
```

The example illustrates a couple of use cases of a class with a reference inside. We can create such objects and make copies, but we cannot assign new values or rebind a reference.

However, having a reference is not uncommon, and you might implicitly create such types when you use lambdas. Have a look:

```cpp
#include <iostream>
#include <string>

int main() {
    std::string str { "Name"};
    auto changeStr = [&str](int x) {
        str = std::to_string(x);
    };
    std::cout << str << '\n';
    changeStr(10);
    std::cout << str << '\n';
}
```

If we see that code through C++Insights, which exposes "how the compiler changes the code", we can see the following "unnamed" class created from the lambda:

```cpp
// basic string<> translated to std::string for simplicity...
class __lambda_6_22 {
    public:
    inline /*constexpr */ void operator()(int x) const {
      str.operator=(std::to_string(x));
    }
    __lambda_6_22(std::string & _str) : str{_str} { }
    private:
    std::string & str;
  };
```

See @C++Insights[7].

Changing to `std::reference_wrapper`

Having a regular reference might bring some complications to your class design. As an alternative approach, the C++ Standard Library gives us `std::reference_wrapper` that "wraps a reference in a copyable, assignable object".

See the example:

---

[7]https://cppinsights.io/s/82fbe838

```cpp
class WrapperWitStdhRef {
    std::reference_wrapper<std::string> name_;
public:
    explicit WrapperWitStdhRef(std::string& n) : name_(n) { }
    const std::string& name() const { return name_; }
    void rebind(std::string& name) { name_ = name; }
    void name(const std::string& name) { name_.get() = name; }
};

int main() {
    std::string str { "Name"};
    WrapperWitStdhRef w { str };
    w.name(str);
    WrapperWitStdhRef x { w };
    std::cout << "str:      " << str << '\n';
    std::cout << "x.name(): " << x.name() << '\n';
    x.name("abc");
    std::cout << "str:      " << str << '\n';
    std::cout << "x.name(): " << x.name() << '\n';
    //WrapperWitStdhRef def {}; // cannot default construct
    x = w; // fine now
}
```

We have a very similar code this time, but notice two member functions: name() and rebind(). To change the value pointer by name_, you need to use the .get() member function. The regular assignment operator rebinds the reference. Same as before, the class is still not default-constructible as reference_wrapper cannot be empty/null.

Other use cases for reference_wrapper:

- Storing std::reference_wrapper in containers,
- Creating pairs or tuples of references,
- Passing reference-like arguments to the start function of std::thread.

 std::refrence_wrapper is usually implemented as a raw pointer to the wrapped type. Extra member functions and operators make it "feel" like a reference type that can also rebind.

Summary

In this chapter, we covered several categories of data members that expose some interesting properties. Thanks to type traits from the Standard Library, we can have a quick test showing the properties of such classes. The core function is:

Ex 10.8. Showing basic properties of a type. Run @Compiler Explorer

```
template <typename T> void ShowProps() {
    cout << typeid(T).name() << " props: \n";
    cout << "default constructible " << is_default_constructible_v<T>;
    cout << " | copy assignable " << is_copy_assignable_v<T> << " | ";
    cout << "move assignable " << is_move_assignable_v<T> << '\n';
    cout << "copy constructible " << is_copy_constructible_v<T> << " | ";
    cout << "move constructible " << is_move_constructible_v<T> << '\n';
}
```

Using the above function template, I generated the following table:

Non-static data member type	Default constructor	Copy constructor	Copy assign	Move constructor	Move assign
Copyable, assignable, „regular"	Yes	Default	Default	Default	Default
const	No, unless default value set	Default	Custom only	Default	Custom only
Raw pointer	Yes	Default (shallow!)	Default (shallow!)	Default	Default
std::unique_ptr	Yes	Custom only	Custom only	Default	Default
std::shared_ptr	Yes	Default, shallow, but might be safe	Default, shallow, but might be safe	Default	Default
Reference	No	Default (shallow!)	Custom only	Default	Custom only
std::reference_wrapper	No	Default (shallow!)	Default (shallow!)	Default	Default

Non-regular data members summary

For example, when your class has a `const` data member, then the default constructor is not available (unless you assign some default value), the copy and the move constructors can be provided by the compiler, but default assignment operators are not available. "Custom only" means that the compiler cannot generate a default implementation, and the user has to provide some custom implementation.

Having discussed other categories of non-static data members, we can now examine static data members. How to use them in Modern C++? See the next chapter.

11. Non-local objects

Thus far, we considered variables that appeared in some local function scope or as sub-objects of a class type. However, this is not the only option, and C++ allows us to declare various forms of non-local objects: they usually live throughout the execution of the whole program. In this chapter, we'll look at global variables, static data members, and thread-local objects. We'll also consider new features for safe initialization from C++17 and C++20.

Storage duration and linkage

To start, we need to understand two key properties of an object in C++: *storage* and *linkage*. Let's begin with the definition of *storage*, from [basic.stc#general[1]]:

> The storage duration is the property of an object that defines the minimum potential lifetime of the storage containing the object. The storage duration is determined by the construct used to create the object.

An object in C++ has one of the following storage duration options:

Storage duration	Explanation
automatic	Automatic means that the storage is allocated at the start of the scope. Most local variables have automatic storage duration (except those declared as `static`, `extern`, or `thread_local`).
static	The storage for an object is allocated when the program begins (usually before the `main()` function starts) and deallocated when the program ends. There's only one instance of such an object in the whole program.
thread	The storage for an object is tied to a thread: it's started when a thread begins and is deallocated when the thread ends. Each thread has its own "copy" of that object.
dynamic	The storage for an object is allocated and deallocated using explicit dynamic memory allocation functions. For example, by the call to `new`/`delete`.

[1]https://timsong-cpp.github.io/cppwp/n4868/basic.stc#general

And the definition for the second property: *linkage*, extracted from [basic.link[2]]:

> A name is said to have linkage when it can denote the same object, reference, function, type, template, namespace, or value as a name introduced by a declaration in another scope.

We have several linkage types:

Linkage	Explanation
external linkage	External means that the name can be referred to from the scopes in the same or other translation units. Non-const global variables have external linkage by default.
module linkage	Available since C++20. A name can be referred in scopes of the same module or module units.
internal linkage	A name can be referred to from the scopes in the same translation units. For example, a `static`, `const`, and `constexpr` global variables have internal linkage.
no linkage	Cannot be referred from other scopes.
language linkage	Allows interoperability between different programming languages, usually with C. For example, by declaring `extern "C"`.

If we work with regular variables declared in a function's scope, the storage is automatic, and there's no linkage, but those properties matter for objects in a global or thread scope. In the following sections, we'll try experiments with global objects to understand the meaning of those definitions.

Static duration and external linkage

Consider the following code:

---

[2] https://timsong-cpp.github.io/cppwp/n4868/basic.link#2

Ex 11.1. Static and automatic objects. Run @Compiler Explorer

```
#include <iostream>

struct Value {
    Value(int x) : v(x) { std::cout << "Value(" << v << ")\n"; }
    ~Value() noexcept { std::cout << "~Value(" << v << ")\n"; }

    int v {0};
};

Value v{42};

int main() {
    puts("main starts...");
    Value x { 100 };
    puts("main ends...");
}
```

If we run the example, you'll see the following output:

```
Value(42)
main starts...
Value(100)
main ends...
~Value(100)
~Value(42)
```

In the example, there's a structure called Value, and I declare and define a global variable v. As you can see from the output, the object is initialized **before** the main() function starts and is destroyed after the main() ends.

The global variable v has a static storage duration and external linkage. On the other hand, the second variable, x, has no linkage and automatic storage duration (as it's a local variable).

If we have two translation units: main.cpp and other.cpp, we can point to the same global variable by declaring and defining an object in one place and then using the extern keyword to provide the declaration in the other translation unit. This is illustrated by the following example:

Ex 11.2. Static and extern. Run @Wandbox

```cpp
// main.cpp
#include <iostream>
#include "value.h"

Value v{42};
void foo();

int main() {
    std::cout << "in main(): " << &v << '\n';
    foo();
    std::cout << "main ends...\n";
}

// other.cpp
#include "value.h"

extern Value v; // declaration only!

void foo() {
    std::cout << "in foo(): " << &v << '\n';
}
```

If we run the code, you'll see that the address of v is the same in both lines. For instance:

```
Value(42)
in main(): 0x404194
in foo(): 0x404194
main ends...
~Value(42)
```

Internal linkage

If you want two global variables visible as separate objects in each translation unit, you need to define them as `static`. This will change their linkage from external to internal.

Ex 11.3. Static and internal linkage. Run @Wandbox

```cpp
// main.cpp
#include <iostream>
#include "value.h"

static Value v{42};
void foo();

int main() {
    std::cout << "in main(): " << &v << '\n';
    foo();
    std::cout << "main ends...\n";
}

// other.cpp
#include "value.h"

static Value v { 100 };

void foo() {
    std::cout << "in foo(): " << &v << '\n';
}
```

Now, you have two different objects which live in the static storage (outside `main()`):

```
Value(42)
Value(100)
in main(): 0x404198
in foo(): 0x4041a0
main ends...
~Value(100)
~Value(42)
```

You can also achieve this by wrapping objects in an anonymous namespace:

```
namespace {
    Value v{42};
}
```

Additionally, if you declare `const Value v{42};` in one translation unit, then `const` implies an internal linkage. If you want to have a `const` object with the external linkage, you need to add the `extern` keyword:

```
// main.cpp:
extern const Value v { 42 }; // declaration and definition!

// other.cpp:
extern const Value v; // declaration
```

While constant global variables might be useful, try to avoid mutable global objects. They complicate the program's state and may introduce subtle bugs or data races, especially in multithreaded programs. In this chapter, we cover all global variables so that you can understand how they work, but use them carefully. See this C++ Core Guideline: I.2: Avoid non-const global variables[3].

Thread local storage duration

Since C++11, you can use a new keyword, `thread_local`, to indicate the special storage of a variable. A `thread_local` object can be declared at a local scope or at a global scope. In both cases, its initialization is tied to a thread, and the storage is located in the Thread Local Storage space[4]. Each thread that uses this object creates a copy of it.

---

[3]https://isocpp.github.io/CppCoreGuidelines/CppCoreGuidelines#i2-avoid-non-const-global-variables
[4]See more at https://en.wikipedia.org/wiki/Thread-local_storage

Ex 11.4. Example of thread_local variables. Run @Compiler Explorer

```cpp
#include <iostream>
#include <thread>
#include <mutex>

std::mutex mutPrint;
thread_local int x = 0;

void foo() {
    thread_local int y = 0;
    std::lock_guard guard(mutPrint);
    std::cout << "in thread\t" << std::this_thread::get_id() << " ";
    std::cout << "&x " << &x << ", ";
    std::cout << "&y " << &y << '\n';
}

int main() {
    std::cout << "main\t" << std::this_thread::get_id() << " &x " << &x << '\n';

    std::jthread worker1 { foo };
    foo();
    std::jthread worker2 { foo };
    foo();
}
```

And here's a possible output:

```
main       4154632640 &x 0xf7a2a9b8
in thread  4154632640 &x 0xf7a2a9b8, &y 0xf7a2a9bc
in thread  4154628928 &x 0xf7a29b38, &y 0xf7a29b3c
in thread  4154632640 &x 0xf7a2a9b8, &y 0xf7a2a9bc
in thread  4146236224 &x 0xf7228b38, &y 0xf7228b3c
```

The example uses a mutex `mutPrint` to synchronize printing to the output. First, inside `main()`, you can see the ID of the main thread and the address of the x variable. Later in the output, you can see that `foo()` was called, and it's done in the main thread (compare the IDs). As you can see, the addresses of x are the same because it's the same thread. On the other hand, later in the output, we can see an invocation from two different threads; in both cases, the addresses of x and y are different. In summary, we have three distinct copies of x and three of y.

From the example above, we can also spot that across a single thread, `thread_local` in a function scope behaves like a `static` local variable. What's more, the two lines are equivalent:

```
// local or global scope...
static thread_local int x;
thread_local int y;          // means the same as above
```

 The code uses `std::jthread` from C++20, which automatically joins to the caller thread when the `jthread` object goes out of scope. When you use `std::thread` you need to call `join()` manually.

Thread local variables might be used when you want a shared global state, but keep it only for a given thread and thus avoid synchronization issues. To simulate such behavior and understand those types of variables, we can create a map of variables:

```
std::map<thread_id, Object> objects;
```

And each time you access a global variable, you need to access it via the current thread id, something like:

```
objects[std::this_thread::get_id()] = x; // modify the global object...
```

Of course, the above code is just a simplification, and thanks to `thread_local`, all details are hidden by the compiler, and we can safely access and modify objects.

In another example, we can observe when each copy is created, have a look:

Ex 11.5. Begin and end of a thread-local variable. Run @Compiler Explorer

```
#include <iostream>
#include <thread>
#include "value.h"

thread_local Value x { 42 };

void foo() {
    std::cout << "foo()\n";
    x.v = 100;
}

int main() {
    std::cout << "main " << std::this_thread::get_id() << '\n';
    {
        std::jthread worker1 { foo };
        std::jthread worker2 { foo };
    }
    std::cout << "end main()\n";
}
```

Possible output:

```
main 4154399168
foo()
Value(42)
foo()
Value(42)
~Value(~Value(100)
100)
end main()
```

This time the variable x prints a message from its constructor and destructor, and thus we can see some details. Only two `foo` thread workers use this variable, and we have two copies, not three (the main thread doesn't use the variable). Each copy starts its lifetime when its parent thread starts and ends when the thread joins into the main thread.

As an experiment, you can try commenting out the line with `x.v = 100`. After the compilation, you won't see any `Value` constructor or destructor calls. It's because the object is not used by any thread, and thus no object is created.

Possible use cases:

- Having a random number generator, one per thread
- One thread processes a server connection and stores some state across
- Keeping some statistics per thread, for example, to measure load in a thread pool.

Dynamic storage duration

For completeness, we also have to mention dynamic storage duration. In short, by requesting a memory through explicit calls to memory management routines, you have full control when the object is created and destroyed. In most basic scenario you can call `new()` and then `delete`:

```cpp
auto pInt = new int{42}; // only for illustration...
auto pSmartInt = std::make_unique<int>(42);
int main() {
    auto pDouble = new double { 42.2 }; // only for illustration...
    // use pInt...
    // use pDouble
    delete pInt;
    delete pDouble;
}
```

The above artificial example showed three options for dynamic storage:

- `pInt` is a non-local object initialized with the new expression. We have to destroy it manually; in this case, it's at the end of the `main()` function.
- `pDouble` is a local variable that is also dynamically initialized; we also have to delete it manually.
- On the other hand, `pSmartInt` is a smart pointer, a `std::unique_ptr` that is dynamically initialized. Thanks to the RAII pattern, there's no need to manually delete the memory, as the smart pointer will automatically do it when it goes out of scope. In our case, it will be destroyed after `main()` shuts down.

Dynamic memory management is very tricky, so it's best to rely on RAII and smart pointers to clean the memory. The example above used raw new and delete only to show the basic usage, but in production code, try to avoid it. See more in those resources: 6 Ways to Refactor new/delete into unique ptr - C++ Stories[5] and 5 ways how unique_ptr enhances resource safety in your code - C++ Stories[6].

We spoke about memory deallocation and resource handling in the Destructor chapter; you can find more information there.

Initialization of non-local static objects

All non-local objects are initialized before `main()` starts and before their first "use". But there's more to that.

Consider the following code:

Ex 11.6. Static initialization. Run @Compiler Explorer

```cpp
#include <iostream>

struct Value { /*as before*/ };

double z = 100.0;
int x;
Value v{42};

int main() {
    puts("main starts...");
    std::cout << x << '\n';
    puts("main ends...");
}
```

All global objects z, x, and v are initialized during the program startup and before the `main()` starts. We can divide the initialization into two distinct types: *static initialization* and *dynamic initialization*.

The static initialization occurs in two forms:

---
[5]https://www.cppstories.com/2021/refactor-into-uniqueptr/
[6]https://www.cppstories.com/2017/12/why-uniqueptr/

- **constant initialization** - this happens for the z variable, which is value initialized from a constant expression.
- The x object looks uninitialized, but for non-local static objects, the compiler performs **zero initialization**, which means they will take the value of zero (and then it's converted to the appropriate type). Pointers are set to `nullptr`, arrays, trivial structs, and unions have their members initialized to a zero value.

Don't rely on zero initialization for static objects. Always try to assign some value to be sure of the outcome. In the book, I only showed it so you could see the whole picture.

Now, v global objects are initialized during so-called **dynamic initialization** of non-local variables". It happens for objects that cannot be constant initialized or zero-initialized during static initialization at the program startup.

In a single translation unit, the order of dynamic initialization of global variables (including static data members) is well defined. If you have multiple compilation units, then the order is unspecified. When a global object A defined in one compilation unit depends on another global object B defined in a different translation unit, you'll have undefined behavior. Such a problem is called the "static initialization order fiasco"; read more C++ Super FAQ[7].

In short, each static non-local object has to be initialized at the program startup. However, the compiler tries to optimize this process and, if possible, do as much work at compile time. For example, for built-in types initialized from constant expressions, the value of the variable might be stored as a part of the binary and then only loaded during the program startup. If it's not possible, then a dynamic initialization must happen, meaning that the value is computed once before the `main()` starts. Additionally, the compiler might even defer the dynamic initialization until the first use of the variable but must guarantee the program's correctness. Since C++11, we can try to move dynamic initialization to the compile-time stage thanks to `constexpr` (allowing us to write custom types). Since C++20, we can use `constinit` to guarantee constant initialization.

For more information, have a look at this good blog post for more information: C++ - Initialization of Static Variables by Pablo Arias[8] and also a presentation by Matt Godbolt: CppCon 2018 "The Bits Between the Bits: How We Get to main()"[9].

---

[7]https://isocpp.org/wiki/faq/ctors#static-init-order
[8]https://pabloariasal.github.io/2020/01/02/static-variable-initialization/
[9]https://www.youtube.com/watch?v=dOfucXtyEsU

`constinit` in C++20

As discussed in the previous section, it's best to rely on constant initialization if you really need a global variable. In the case of dynamic initialization, the order of initialization might be hard to guess and might cause issues. Consider the following example:

Ex 11.7. Static initialization order fiasco, point.h. Run @Wandbox

```cpp
// point.h
struct Point {
    double x, y;
};
```

Ex 11.7. Static initialization order fiasco, a.cpp. Run @Wandbox

```cpp
// a.cpp
#include <iostream>
#include "point.h"

extern Point center;
Point offset = { center.x + 100, center.y + 200};

void foo() {
    std::cout << offset.x << ", " << offset.y << '\n';
}
```

Ex 11.7. Static initialization order fiasco, b.cpp. Run @Wandbox

```cpp
// b.cpp
#include "point.h"

Point createPoint(double x, double y) {
    return Point { x, y };
}

Point center = createPoint(100, 200); //dynamic
```

And the main:

Ex 11.7. Static initialization order fiasco, main.cpp. Run @Wandbox

```
void foo();

int main() {
    foo();
}
```

If we compile this code using the following command and order:

```
$ g++ prog.cc -Wall -Wextra -std=c++2a -pedantic a.cpp b.cpp
```

We'll get the following:

```
100, 200
```

But if you compile b.cpp first and then a.cpp:

```
$ g++ prog.cc -Wall -Wextra -std=c++2a -pedantic b.cpp a.cpp
```

You'll get the following:

```
200, 400
```

There's a dependency of global variables: offset depends on center. If the compilation unit with center were compiled first, the dynamic initialization would be performed, and center would have 100, 200 assigned. Otherwise, it's only zero-initialized, and thus offset has the value of 100, 200.

 This is only a toy example, but imagine a production code! In that case, you might have a hard-to-find bug that comes not from some incorrect computation logic but from the compilation order in the project!

To mitigate the issue, you can apply constinit on the center global variable. This new keyword for C++20 forces constant initialization. In our case, it will ensure that no matter the order of compilation, the value will already be present. What's more, as opposed to constexpr we only force initialization, and the variable itself is not constant. So you can change it later.

Ex 11.8. Constinit approach, b.cpp Run @Wandbox

```cpp
// b.cpp:
#include "point.h"

constexpr Point createPoint(double x, double y) {
    return Point { x, y };
}
constinit Point center = createPoint(100, 200); // constant
```

Please notice that `createPoint` has to be `constexpr` now. The main requirement for `constinit` is that it requires the initializer expression to be evaluated at compile-time, so not all code can be converted that way.

Here's another example that summarizes how to use `constinit`:

Ex 11.8. Constinit std::pair. Run @Compiler Explorer

```cpp
#include <iostream>
#include <utility>

constinit std::pair<int, double> global { 42, 42.2 };
constexpr std::pair<int, double> constG { 42, 42.2 };

int main() {
    std::cout << global.first << ", " << global.second << '\n';
    // but allow to change later...
    global = { 10, 10.1 };
    std::cout << global.first << ", " << global.second << '\n';
    // constG = { 10, 10.1 }; // not allowed, const
}
```

In the above example, I create a global `std::pair` object and force it to use constant initialization. I can do that on all types with `constexpr` constructors or trivial types. Notice that inside `main()`, I can change the value of my object, so it's not `const`. For comparison, I also included the `constG` object, which is a `constexpr` variable. In that case, we'll also force the compiler to use constant initialization, but this time the object cannot be changed later.

 While a `constinit` variable will be constant initialized, it cannot be later used in the initializer of another `constinit` variable. A `constinit` object, is not `constexpr`.

Static variables in a function scope

As you may know, C++ also offers another type of static variable: those defined in a function scope:

```
void foo() {
    static int counter = 0;
    ++counter;
}
```

Above, the counter variable will be initialized and created when foo() is invoked for the first time. In other words, a static local variable is initialized lazily. The counter is kept "outside" the function's stack space. This allows, for example, to keep the state, but limit the visibility of the global object.

Ex 11.9. Counter as a local static variable. Run @Compiler Explorer

```
#include <iostream>

int foo() {
    static int counter = 0;
    return ++counter;
}

int main() {
    foo();
    foo();
    foo();
    auto finalCounter = foo();
    std::cout << finalCounter;
}
```

If you run the program, you'll get 4 as the output.

Static local variables, since C++11, are guaranteed to be initialized in a thread-safe way. The object will be initialized only once if multiple threads enter a function with such a variable. Have a look below:

Ex 11.10. Thread safe static variable initialization. Run @Compiler Explorer

```cpp
#include <iostream>
#include <thread>

struct Value {
    Value(int x) : v(x) { std::cout << "Value(" << v << ")\n"; }
    ~Value() noexcept { std::cout << "~Value(" << v << ")\n"; }

    int v { 0 };
};

void foo() {
    static Value x { 10 };
}

int main() {
    std::jthread worker1 { foo };
    std::jthread worker2 { foo };
    std::jthread worker3 { foo };
}
```

The example creates three threads that call the `foo()` simple function.

However, on GCC, you can also try compiling with the following flags:

```
-std=c++20 -lpthread -fno-threadsafe-statics
```

And then the output might be as follows:

```
Value(Value(1010)
)
Value(10)
~Value(10)
~Value(10)
~Value(10)
```

Three static objects are created now!

We'll address an interesting technique related to those function static objects in the Techniques chapter: the Meyers Singleton section.

About static data members

In general, each and every instance (object) of a class has non-static data members as its own data fields. Each example is separate from the other. If we consider a type (a class) representing a Fruit and it has a data member named "mass", then each particular instance of that Fruit class has a "mass" member belonging to it. If we have 10 Fruit objects, the "mass" data member is replicated ten times. On the other hand, each type can also have static data members that are not bound to any instance of the class. In the case of our Fruit class, we can specify a so-called static variable named "default mass", accessible to each Fruit instance, but it wouldn't be part of any instance. In other words, it's like a global variable in the namespace of the Fruit type.

Consider the following example:

Ex 11.11. Simple `static` Data Member. Run @Compiler Explorer

```
#include <iostream>

struct Value {
    int x;
    static int y; // declaration
};

int Value::y = 0; // definition

int main() {
    Value v { 10 };
    std::cout << "sizeof(int): " << sizeof(int) << '\n';
    std::cout << "sizeof(Value): " << sizeof(Value) << '\n';
    std::cout << "v.x: " << v.x << '\n';
    Value::y = 10;
    std::cout << "Value::y: " << Value::y << '\n';
}
```

When you run this program, you'll see the following output:

```
sizeof(int): 4
sizeof(Value): 4
v.x: 10
Value::y: 10
```

`static int y` declared in the scope of the `Value` class created a variable that is not part of any `Value` type instance. You can see that it doesn't contribute to the size of the whole class. It's the same as the size of the `int` type.

To be precise, `Value::y` has a static storage duration and external linkage.

 Local classes or unnamed classes cannot have static data members.

Here's an example that illustrates the lifetime of a static data member:

Ex 11.12. `static` Data Member Lifetime. Run @Compiler Explorer

```
#include <iostream>

struct Value {
    Value(int x) : v(x) { std::cout << "Value(" << v << ")\n"; }
    ~Value() noexcept { std::cout << "~Value(" << v << ")\n"; }

    int v {0};
};

struct Test {
    Test() { puts("Test::Test()"); }
    ~Test() noexcept { puts("Test::~Test()"); }

    static Value u;
    static Value v;
    static int w;
    static double z;
};

Value Test::v { 42 };
Value Test::u { 24 };
```

```
int Test::w;
double Test::z = 10.5f;

int main() {
    puts("main starts...");
    Test x;
    std::cout << Test::w << '\n';
    std::cout << Test::z << '\n';
    puts("main ends...");
}
```

The code has the Value structure that has two instances in the form of two static data members inside the Test class. Additionally, we have two other data members, w and z, which are built-in types. If we run the code, you'll see the following output:

```
Value(42)
Value(24)
main starts...
Test::Test()
0
10.5
main ends...
Test::~Test()
~Value(24)
~Value(42)
```

As you can see, two Value objects are created before the main starts, in the order of definitions in a file (not declarations!). After the main() function ends, the two objects are destroyed in reverse order.

Motivation for inline variables

In C++11/14, if you wanted to add a static data member to a class, you needed to declare it and define it later in one compilation unit. In the examples from the previous section, we defined it in the same compilation unit as the main() function. Commonly, such variables are defined in the corresponding implementation file.

For example:

Ex 11.13. Static data member, multiple files. Run @Wandbox

```cpp
// a header file:
struct OtherType {
    static int classCounter;

    // ...
};

// implementation, cpp file
int OtherType::classCounter = 0;
```

This time I used Wandbox online compiler - as it's easy to create and compile multiple files:

```
#include <iostream>
#include "othertype.h"

int main() {
    std::cout << __FILE__ << '\n';
    std::cout << "Main starting...\n";
    std::cout << OtherType::classCounter;
}
```

```
$ g++ prog.cc -Wall -Wextra -std=gnu++2b
```

```
prog.cc
Main starting...
0
```

Exit Code: 0

As you can see above, `classCounter` is an `int`, and you have to write it twice: in a header file and then in the CPP file.

```
            header file *.h                  implementation file *.cpp

        struct OtherType {
            static int classCounter;         int OtherType::classCounter = 0;
        };
                        declaration                         definition
```

The only exception to this rule (even before C++11) is a static constant integral variable that you can declare and initialize in one place:

```
class MyType {
    static const int ImportantValue = 42;
};
```

You do not have to define `ImportantValue` in a CPP file.

Fortunately, C++17 gave us **inline variables**, which means we can define a `static inline` variable inside a class without defining them in a CPP file.

Ex 11.14. Static inline member. Run @Wandbox

```
// a header file, C++17:
struct OtherType {
    static inline int classCounter = 0;
    // ...
};
```

The compiler (and the linker) guarantees precisely one definition of this static variable for all translation units that include the class declaration. Inline variables remain `static` class variables, so they will be initialized before the `main()` function is called.

If we read Dynamic Initialization @C++Reference[10] and C++ Standard: basic.start[11] we get the following rules about the initialization order:

---

[10]https://en.cppreference.com/w/cpp/language/initialization#Dynamic_initialization
[11]https://timsong-cpp.github.io/cppwp/n4868/basic.start.dynamic#3

> Partially-ordered dynamic initialization, which applies to all inline variables that are not an implicitly or explicitly instantiated specialization. If a partially-ordered V is defined before ordered or partially-ordered W in every translation unit, the initialization of V is sequenced before the initialization of W.

Based on the previous code, here's the example with the `Value` class and multiple compilation units:

Ex 11.15. Inline Variables and multiple compilation units, test.h. Run @Wandbox

```cpp
// test.h
#include <iostream>

struct Value {
    Value(int x) : v(x) { std::cout << "Value(" << v << ")\n"; }
    ~Value() noexcept { std::cout << "~Value(" << v << ")\n"; }

    int v {0};
};

struct Test {
    Test() { puts("Test::Test()"); }
    ~Test() noexcept { puts("Test::~Test()"); }

    static inline Value u { 42 };
    static inline Value v { 24 };
};
```

Ex 11.15. Inline Variables and multiple compilation units, main. Run @Wandbox

```cpp
// main.cpp
#include <iostream>
#include "test.h"

void foo();

static Value local{100};

int main() {
    std::cout << "Main starting...\n";
    foo();
    Test t;
}
```

Ex 11.15. Inline Variables and multiple compilation units, other and noname. Run @Wandbox

```cpp
// other.cpp
#include "test.h"

static Value local{200};

void foo() {
    std::cout << "foo starting...\n";
    Test t;
}

// noname.cpp
#include "test.h"

static Value local{300};
```

The build command line:

```
$ g++ prog.cc -Wall -Wextra -std=c++2a noname.cpp other.cpp
```

The output:

```
Value(42)
Value(24)
Value(100)
Value(300)
Value(200)
Main starting...
foo starting...
Test::Test()
Test::~Test()
Test::Test()
Test::~Test()
~Value(200)
~Value(300)
~Value(100)
~Value(24)
~Value(42)
```

As you notice, `Value(42)` and `Value(24)`, `inline` variables, are initialized before all other `Value` global objects. Moreover, depending on the command line, `Value(200)` might be created before `Value(300)`.

The Inline variables make it much easier to develop header-only libraries because there's no need to create CPP files for static variables or use hacks to keep them in a header file (for example, by creating static member functions with static variables inside).

See the example below:

```
// CountedType.h
struct CountedType {
    static inline int classCounter = 0;
    // simple counting... only ctor and dtor implemented...
    CountedType() { ++classCounter; }
    ~CountedType() { --classCounter; }
};
```

And the `main()` function:

Ex 11.15. Static inline member. Run @Wandbox

```
#include <iostream>
#include "CountedType.h"

int main() {
    {
        CountedType c0;
        CountedType c1;
        std::cout << CountedType::classCounter << '\n';
    }
    std::cout << CountedType::classCounter << '\n';
}
```

The code above declares `classCounter` inside `CountedType`, which is a static data member. The class is defined in a separate header file. Thanks to C++17, we can declare the variable as `inline`. Then, there's no need to write a corresponding definition later. Without `inline`, the code wouldn't compile.

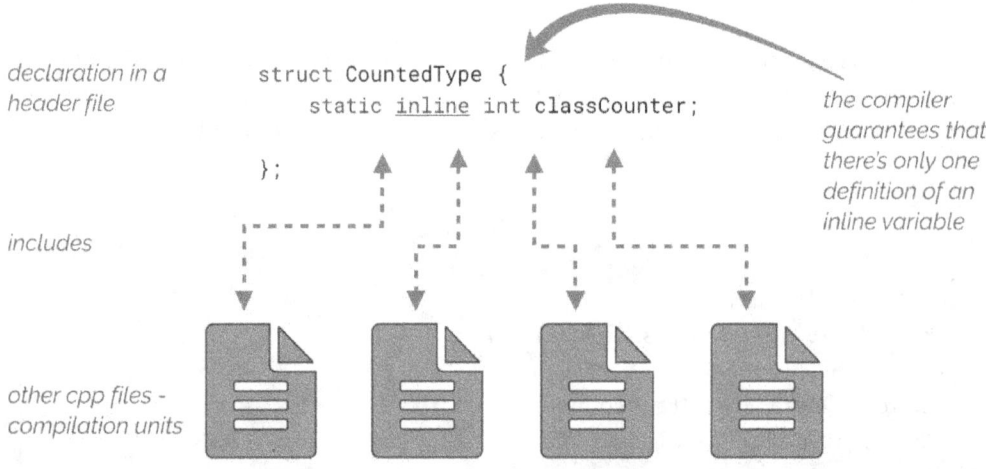

In the `main()` function, the example creates two objects of `CountedType`. The static variable is incremented when there's a call to the constructor. When an object is destroyed, the variable is decremented. We can output this value and see the current count of objects.

The CountedType illustrates an interesting pattern, and we'll extend it to be more usable in the Techniques chapter: the CRTP section.

Global inline variables

While we covered `inline` variables in the context of static data members for a class type, it's not the only use case. As of C++17, you can also declare `inline` variables in the global scope.

Have a look at this basic header file with the declaration and definition of two inline global variables:

```cpp
// globals.h
#include <string>

inline constexpr int gMyGlobal { 10 };
inline const std::string gHelloText {"Hello World "};

// or better in a namespace
namespace appConstants {
    inline constexpr double scalingFactor { 1.33 };
    inline const std::string appName { "Testing app" };
}
```

And you can now use those variables in the `main()`:

Ex 11.17. const global variables. Run @Wandbox

```cpp
// main.cpp
#include <iostream>
#include "globals.h"

int main() {
    std::cout << gMyGlobal << ", " << gHelloText << '\n';
    std::cout << appConstants::scalingFactor << ", "
              << appConstants::appName << '\n';
}
```

Before C++17, you'd had to declare such variables in a header file as `extern`, and provide their definition in one compilation unit. Thanks to C++17, such a use case is now greatly simplified. Please note that having an `inline` variable doesn't solve the static initialization order fiasco, as the order of their dynamic initialization is still not easily predictable across multiple translation units.

Read more about details in this great post from Fluent C++: What Every C++ Developer Should Know to (Correctly) Define Global Constants[12].

`constexpr` and `inline` variables

Throughout the book, we briefly spoke about `constexpr` variables. They are convenient for built-in types like integers and other trivial types. When you apply this keyword to a variable, the compiler might compute its value at compile time and thus save time at runtime.

The compiler automatically implies `inline` when you have a `static constexpr` data member in your class type. See the following example:

```
struct Value {
    static constexpr int basic { 10 };
    static constexpr auto name { "Hello World" };
};
```

When we run this code through C++Insights (run this link[13]), we'll see that the compiler applied `inline` to both of those variables:

```
struct Value {
    inline static constexpr const int basic = {10};
    inline static constexpr const char *const name = {"Hello World"};
};
```

Please remember that implicit `inline` applies only to static class data members. The compiler won't do anything when you declare a global `static constexpr` variable.

---

[12]https://www.fluentcpp.com/2019/07/23/how-to-define-a-global-constant-in-cpp/
[13]https://cppinsights.io/s/a76b8133

Summary

Here are the essential items to remember from this chapter:

- Non-local objects have two fundamental properties: storage duration (where they are stored), and linkage (how we can access them).
- When a non-local object is initialized with a constant expression and the object's constructor is `constexpr` (including built-in types), the initialization may happen at compile time (static initialization).
- If constant initialization (or zero initialization) is not possible, then a static object is initialized in the dynamic initialization stage.
- In a single translation unit, the order of dynamic initialization of non-local variables (including static data members) is performed in the definition order, but it's unspecified across multiple compilation units.
- A static data member is not bound to any class instances.
- A static data member has a static storage duration and external linkage.
- The compiler and the linker ensure there's only one definition of an `inline` variable; there's no need to define and declare such variables in different places.
- The compiler automatically implies `inline` when you have a `static constexpr` data member.

12. Aggregates and Designated Initializers in C++20

Across the book, you've seen a lot of cases for intuitively simple structures with all public data members. Such types, along with arrays, are called *aggregates*. In this chapter, we'll summarize the knowledge and look at some C++20 changes. Moreover, this topic will also be valid in C++23, as in the upcoming language standard, no new things change aggregate behavior [1].

Aggregates as of C++20

As of C++20, here's the definition of *aggregate type* from the Standard: dcl.init.aggr[2].

> An aggregate is an array or a class type with:
> - no user-declared or inherited constructors
> - no private or protected direct non-static data members
> - no virtual functions, and
> - no virtual, private, or protected base classes

Here are some examples of aggregates:

---

[1] See all C++23 language features at: https://en.cppreference.com/w/cpp/compiler_support#cpp23
[2] https://timsong-cpp.github.io/cppwp/n4868/dcl.init.aggr#:initialization,aggregate

Ex 12.1. Aggregate classes. Run @Compiler Explorer

```cpp
struct Base { int x { 42 }; };
struct Derived : Base { int y; };

struct Param {
    std::string name;
    int val;
    void Parse();
};

int main() {
    Derived d { 100, 1000 };
    std::cout << "d.x " << d.x << ", d.y " << d.y << '\n';
    Derived d2 { 1 };
    std::cout << "d2.x " << d2.x << ", d2.y " << d2.y << '\n';
    Param p { "value", 10 };
    std::cout << "p.name " << p.name << ", p.val " << p.val << '\n';

    double arr[] { 1.1, 2.2, 3.3, 4.4};
    std::cout << "arr[0] " << arr[0] << '\n';
    std::array floats { 10.1f, 20.2f, 30.3f };
    std::cout << "floats[0] " << floats[0] << '\n';
    std::array params {Param{"val", 10}, Param{"name", 42}};
    std::cout << "params[0].name " << params[0].name << '\n';
}
```

Let's investigate some of the lines above:

- d is of the Derived type and initializes d.x to 100 and d.y to 1000.
- d2 has an initializer only for d.x, but d.y will be value initialized.
- Param has a member function, but this is allowed, and there are no issues with initializing the p object.
- arr is another example of an aggregate which is an array. The compiler can deduce the number of elements for the array.
- floats is std::array which is a moder C++ version, from the Standard Library. Thanks to CTAD compiler deduces the type of the array and the number of elements.

Brace elision and sub-aggregates

Consider the following case with a custom structure that holds an aggregate:

```
struct Point3D { int coords[3] };
```

The complete form of initialization of objects of the above class looks as follows:

```
Point3D center { {100, 100, 100 } };
```

The first pair of braces opens the initialization of the Point3D structure, and then we open another pair of braces for the array. In C++, we can, however, skip the extra braces and rely on *brace elision* and write:

```
Point3D center { 100, 100, 100 };
```

From the C++ Standard: *dcl.init.aggr*[3]:

> If the initializer-list begins with a left brace, then the succeeding comma-separated list of initializer-clauses initializes the elements of a subaggregate; it is erroneous for there to be more initializer-clauses than elements. If, however, the initializer-list for a subaggregate does not begin with a left brace, then only enough initializer-clauses from the list are taken to initialize the elements of the subaggregate; any remaining initializer-clauses are left to initialize the next element of the aggregate of which the current subaggregate is an element.

For our center variable, we can see that the first pair of braces begins initializing the whole object. And later, there's no other left brace, so the compiler consumes init-clauses for all array elements.

However, brace elision might sometimes cause some headaches. Consider the following[4]:

---

[3] https://timsong-cpp.github.io/cppwp/n4868/dcl.init.aggr#15
[4] Thanks to prof. Boguslaw Cyganek for the topic and the example ideas.

Ex 12.2. Brace elision issues. Run @Compiler Explorer

```
struct Array { double data[2]; }
struct Matrix { Array arr[2]; }

Matrix mat1 { 1, 2, 3, 4 };              // fine
Matrix mat2 { { 1, 2, 3, 4 } };          // fine
Matrix mat3 { { {1, 2}, {3, 4} } };      // fine, full form
Matrix mat4 { {1, 2}, {3, 4} };          // doesn't compile!
```

Let's expand the code:

- `mat1` uses full brace elision. The first brace opens the initialization, and since there are no other braces, the compiler reads numbers and fills `arr[0].data[0]`, then `arr[0].data[1]`, and later `arr[0].data` elements end, so the compiler moves to `arr[1].data[0]` and `arr[1].data[1]`.
- `mat2` has two left braces, but the effect is the same as for `mat`. The compiler sees the second left brace and starts the initialization of the `mat.arr` sub-object.
- `mat3` is the complete initialization form, with all braces.

The line with `mat4` does not compile! Clang or GCC will report issues about `too many initializers for 'Matrix'`.

The most outer braces `{ }` represent the initializer for the `Matrix` structure. Then we open another left brace `{`. While we treat it like the brace only for `arr[0]`, the compiler, according to the rules, takes the initializer for the whole `arr` sub-aggregate (as in `mat2`). That's why 1 and 2 goes to `arr[0]`, but then, with the right brace `}`, the compiler ends the initialization by setting 0, 0 to `arr[1]`. Now it sees `{3, 4}` and has more initializers than needed. In other words, the compiler considers the expression as:

```
Matrix mat5 { {1, 2} }; // fine, mat5 is 1, 2, 0, 0
```

Brace elision is a handy way to save some typing. Still, it's good to understand how it works to avoid confusion that might appear from complex syntax.

Round parens in C++20

In C++20, in some limited cases, you can also use parens X(args...) to initialize an aggregate. Here's a short example with major use cases and limitations:

Ex 12.3. Initialization with round parens in C++20. Run @Compiler Explorer

```cpp
struct Point { int x; int y; };
struct PointExt { Point pt; int z; };

int main() {
    Point pt (1, 2);
    // Point pt = (1, 2);   // doesn't work with "copy" syntax
    Point pt1 = {1, 2};     // fine with braces

    //Point pt2 { 1.1, 2.2 }; // narrowing prevented
    Point pt3 ( 1.1, 2.2 );   // narrowing is fine

    PointExt pt4 { 4, 5, 6};          // brace elision works
    // PointExt pt5 ( (4, 5), 6);     // nesting doesn't work
    // PointExt pt5 ( 4, 5, 6);       // brace elision doesn't work
    PointExt pt5 ( Point(4, 5), 6); // need to be explicit

    double params[] (9.81, 3.14, 1.44);
    // double paramsDeduced[] = (9.81, 3.14, 1.44); // wrong syntax
    int arrX[10]  (1, 2, 3, 4); // fine, rest is 0
}
```

Here are some basic rules about the new way of initialization:
- You have to use direct initialization (args...) not copy style =(args...). In the example, pt = (1, 2); fails to compile, while Point pt1 = {1, 2}; works. A similar rule works for arrays.
- On the other hand, braces {} prevent narrowing conversion, but parens () allows it. In the example, pt3 will be initialized with 1 and 2, which are truncated from 1.1 and 2.2 double values.
- When you use braces, you can skip braces for nested types. This feature is impossible with parens, and you must be explicit about sub-objects.

Such improvement helps, especially in a generic template code where you want to work with various types of objects. For example, the following code wasn't possible until C++20:

Ex 12.4. Aggregates and parens for `make_unique`. Run @Compiler Explorer

```cpp
struct Point { int x; int y; };

int main() {
    auto ptr = std::make_unique<Point>(10, 20);
}
```

make_unique takes a variable number of arguments and passes them to a constructor. This function uses parens to call the constructor. Since our aggregate has no user-declared constructors, then such syntax generates errors. With the C++20 change, the code works fine now.

We can also try another example that compiles in C++20 but failed before:

Ex 12.5. Aggregates and parens for `emplace_`. Run @Compiler Explorer

```cpp
struct Point { int x; int y; };

int main() {
    std::vector<Point> points;
    points.emplace_back(10, 20);
}
```

The emplace_back() function takes arguments and creates a Point object at the end of the vector. This is an alternative to push_back, which requires passing an already created object, and then a copy of the object is put at the end of the container. emplace_back uses () to create an object, and before C++20 aggregates had issues to work with this function.

If you like to know more, I highly recommend reading C++20's parenthesized aggregate initialization has some downsides – Arthur O'Dwyer[5], which discusses pros and cons of this new initialization syntax. Plus, look at this short lighting talk from ACCU 2022 by Timur Doumler: Lightning Talk - Direct Aggregate Initialisation[6].

---

[5]https://quuxplusone.github.io/blog/2022/06/03/aggregate-parens-init-considered-kinda-bad/
[6]https://www.youtube.com/watch?v=1_2e8r4zXJg

The basics of designated initializers

The C++20 Standard also gives us another handy way to initialize data members. The new feature is called designated initializers, which might be familiar to C programmers.

As of C++20, to initialize an aggregate object, you can write the following:

```
Type obj = { .designator = val, .designator { val2 }, ... };
```

For example:

```
struct Point { double x; double y; };
Point p { .x = 10.0, .y = 20.0 };
```

Designator points to a name of a non-static data member from our class, like .x or .y.

One of the main reasons to use this new kind of initialization is to increase readability. Compare the following initialization forms:

```
struct Date {
    int year;
    int month;
    int day;
};

// new
Date inFutureCpp20 { .year = 2050, .month = 4, .day = 10 };
// old
Date inFutureOld   { 2050, 4, 10 };
```

In the case of the Date class, it might be unclear what the order of days/month or month/days is. With designated initializers (inFutureCpp20), it's very easy to see the order of data members.

Rules for designated initializers

The following rules apply to designated initializers:

- designated initializers work only for aggregate initialization, so they only support aggregate types,
- designated initialization requires braces {} and doesn't support C++20 initialization with parens (),
- designators can only refer to non-static data members,
- designators in the initialization expression must have the same order of data members in a class declaration,
    - this is unlike the C language, where you can put designators in any order,
- not all data members must be specified in the expression,
- you cannot mix regular initialization with designators,
- there can only be one designator for a data member,
- you cannot nest designators.

Here's a simple example that illustrates the main errors with designated initializers:

```
struct Date {
    int year;
    int month;
    int day;
    static int mode;
};

Date d { .mode = 10 };               // error, mode is static!
Date d { .day = 1, .year = 2010 };   // error, out of order!
Date d { 2050, .month = 12 };        // error, mix!
```

The code above illustrates several cases where designated initializers won't work: static data member, use out-of-order initialization, or a mix. In all cases, the compiler generates an error.

Advantages of designated initialization

- Readability: A designator points to the specific data member, so it's impossible to make mistakes here.
- Flexibility: You can skip some data members and rely on default values for others.
- Compatibility with C: In C99, it's popular to use a similar form of initialization (although even more relaxed). With the C++20 feature, it's possible to have very similar code and share it.
- Standardization: Some compilers, like GCC or Clang, already have some extensions for this feature, so it's a natural step to enable it in all compilers.

Examples

Let's take a look at some examples:

Ex 12.6. Designated initializers demo. Run @Compiler Explorer

```cpp
#include <format>
#include <iostream>

struct Product {
    std::string name_;
    bool inStock_ { false };
    double price_ = 0.0;
};
void Print(const Product& p) {
    std::cout << std::format("name: {}, in stock: {}, price: {}\n",
              p.name_, p.inStock_, p.price_);
}
struct Time { int hour; int minute; };
struct Date { Time t; int year; int month; int day; };

int main() {
    Date d { .t { .hour = 10, .minute = 35 },
             .year = 2050, .month = 5, .day = 10 };
    std::cout << std::format("time: {}:{} in {}\n",
              d.t.hour, d.t.minute, d.year);
```

```cpp
    Product p { .name_ = "box", .inStock_ {true }};
    Print(p);
    // pass to a function:
    Print({.name_ = "tv", .inStock_ {true }, .price_{100.0}});
    // not all members used:
    Print({.name_ = "car", .price_{2000.0}});
}
```

It's also interesting that we can use designated initialization inside another designated initialization. For example:

```cpp
struct Time { int hour; int min; };
struct Date { Time t; int year; int month; int day; };

Date d { .t { .hour = 10, .min = 6 }, .year = 2050, .month = 5, .day = 10 };
```

However, we can't use "nested" ones, like:

```cpp
Date d { .t.hour = 10, .t.min = 35, .year = 2050, .month = 5, .day = 10 };
```

The syntax .t.hour does not work.

As another demo, we can create an almost JSON-like structure[7]:

Ex 12.7. JSON-like structure initialization. Run @Compiler Explorer

```cpp
struct Date { int year; int month; int day; };
struct Team { std::string name; std::string where; };
struct GameSession {
    std::string game;
    std::string localization;
    std::vector<Team> teams;
    Date date;
};

int main() {
    GameSession test {
```

---

[7]Thanks to Mariusz Jaskółka for inspiration.

```cpp
        .game = "Pong",
        .localization = "Pacific Ocean",
        .teams  = {
            Team {
                .name = "Johny Test",
                .where = "Arctica",
            },
            Team {
                .name = "Jane Doe",
                .where = "Antarctic",
            },
        },
        .date = {
            .year = 2022,
            .month = 10,
            .day = 6
        },
    };
}
```

Thanks to designated initializers, we can create large objects and still be able to assign values in a readable form. Such `GameSession` from the above demo might be handy for some unit test scenarios.

Summary

When you have a simple type composed of all public data members without complex special member functions, C++ allows you to create them in a simplified manner. What's more, C++ has evolved to streamline the work even more. For example, in C++20, we get Designated Initializers which usually yield a more readable way of initializing aggregate types. Additionally, C++20 extended the use of regular parens () for initialization, so the "factory" function can easily be more generic and work with both aggregate and complex classes.

13. Techniques and Use Cases

Across the book, we've touched on many different topics, sometimes only in a theoretical way. In this chapter, however, I group many of those features and demonstrate their benefits in several practical use cases.

You'll learn about the following aspects:

- Strong types and the `explicit` keyword,
- Initializing string data members,
- Reducing extra copies through `emplace` or `in_place`,
- Copy and Swap Idiom as a potential simplification of copy and move operations,
- CRTP,
- Meyers Singleton
- Factory with self-registering types.

Let's start.

Using `explicit` for strong types

If you recall the first chapter, I used `double` to indicate horsepower (hp) inside the `CarInfo` structure. However, we might quickly encounter a problem where we forget about the unit and treat it as Watts instead. Can we limit such problematic cases?

The answer is positive, and the main idea is to wrap the data member `double power` in a separate class type with `explicit` constructors. That it will be harder to misuse it, such an approach is called *Strong Typing*.

Have a look at two similar wrapper types:

Ex 13.1. Strong types and area units classes. Run @Compiler Explorer

```cpp
constexpr double ToWattsRatio { 745.699872 };

class HorsePower;

class WattPower {
public:
    WattPower() = default;
    explicit WattPower(double p) : power_{p} { }
    explicit WattPower(const HorsePower& h);

    double getValue() const { return power_; }
private:
    double power_ {0.};
};

class HorsePower {
public:
    HorsePower() = default;
    explicit HorsePower(double p) : power_{p} { }
    explicit HorsePower(const WattPower& w);

    double getValue() const { return power_; }
private:
    double power_ {0.};
};
```

As you can see, we have two types that use `explicit` constructors to initialize their private data members. To create an object, you have to write the correct type name explicitly, and thus it should limit the chance of mistakes.

Here is the implementation of the converting constructors as well as stream operators for easy output:

Ex 13.1. Strong Types and area units, implementation. Run @Compiler Explorer

```cpp
constexpr double ToWattsRatio { 745.699872 };

class HorsePower;
class WattPower { /* as before */ };
class HorsePower { /* as before */ };

WattPower::WattPower(const HorsePower& h)
: power_{h.getValue()*ToWattsRatio} { }

HorsePower::HorsePower(const WattPower& w)
: power_{w.getValue()/ToWattsRatio} { }

std::ostream& operator<<(std::ostream& os, const WattPower& w) {
    os << w.getValue() << "W";
    return os;
}
std::ostream& operator<<(std::ostream& os, const HorsePower& h) {
    os << h.getValue() << "hp";
    return os;
}
```

The interface allows us to convert between various units safely.

```cpp
//HorsePower hp = 10.; // not possible, copy initialization
HorsePower hp{ 10. }; // fine
WattPower w { 1. }; // fine
WattPower watts { hp }; // fine, performs the proper conversion for us!
```

Additionally, we have the output support that writes out the proper unit name.

We can use the solution now:

```cpp
struct CarInfo {
    std::string name;
    unsigned year;
    unsigned seats;
    HorsePower power; // << instead of double!
};
void printInfo(const CarInfo& c) {
    std::cout << c.name << ", " << c.year << " year, "
              << c.seats << " seats, "<< c.power << '\n';
}
int main() {
    CarInfo firstCar{"Megane", 2003, 5, HorsePower{116}};
    printInfo(firstCar);
    CarInfo superCar{"Ferrari", 2022, 2, HorsePower{300}};
    printInfo(superCar);
    superCar.power = HorsePower{WattPower{500000}};
    printInfo(superCar);
}
```

And we'll get the following output:

```
Megane, 2003 year, 5 seats, 116hp
Ferrari, 2022 year, 2 seats, 300hp
Ferrari, 2022 year, 2 seats, 670.511hp
```

While I had to be more explicit and write the types, the code is safer as it's harder to type something accidentally.

In C++11, you can also leverage user-defined literals to allow easier creation of objects. Especially useful for units, string, numerical types, time, and dates. For example, we could create a named literal _m2 and then write 50.0_m2 to create an instance rather than SqMeters{50.2}. See more at C++Reference - User-defined literals[1].

For more information about Strong Types, I highly recommend reading many articles on the Fluent C++ blog. For example, start with this one: Strong types for strong interfaces - Fluent C++[2].

---

[1] https://en.cppreference.com/w/cpp/language/user_literal
[2] https://www.fluentcpp.com/2016/12/08/strong-types-for-strong-interfaces/

Best way to initialize `string` data members

See the following example:

```cpp
class UserName {
    std::string name_;
public:
    explicit UserName(const std::string& str) : name_(str) { }
};
```

As you can see, a constructor is taking `const std::string& str`.

Let's compare those alternative implementations in three cases: creating from a string literal, creating from an `lvalue`, and creating from an `rvalue` reference:

```cpp
// creation from a string literal
UserName u1{"John With Very Long Name"};

// creation from lvalue:
std::string s2 {"Marc With Very Long Name"};
UserName u2 { s2 };
// use s2 later...

// from rvalue reference
std::string s3 {"Marc With Very Long Name"};
UserName u3 { std::move(s3) };

// third case is also similar to taking a return value:
std::string GetString() { return "some string..."; }
UserName u4 { GetString() };
```

Please note that allocations/creation of `s2` and `s3` are not taken into account; we're only looking at what happens for the constructor call. For `s2` we can also assume it's used later in the code.

For `const std::string&`:

- `u1` - two allocations: the first one creates a temp string and binds it to the input parameter, and then there's a copy into `name_`.

- u2 - one allocation: we have a no-cost binding to the reference, and then there's a copy into the member variable.
- u3 - one allocation: we have a no-cost binding to the reference, and then there's a copy into the member variable.
- You'd have to write a `ctor` taking rvalue reference to skip one allocation for the `u1` case, and also, that could skip one copy for the `u3` case (since we could move from rvalue reference).

However, since the introduction of move semantics in C++11, it's usually better and safer to pass `string` as a value and then move from it.

For example:

```
class UserName {
    std::string name_;
public:
    explicit UserName(std::string str) : name_(std::move(str)) { }
};
```

Now we have the following results for `std::string + std::move`:

- u1 - one allocation - for the input argument and then one move into the `name_`. It's better than with `const std::string&` where we got two memory allocations in that case.
- u2 - one allocation - we have to copy the value into the argument, and then we can move from it.
- u3 - no allocations, only two move operations - that's better than with `const string&`!

When you pass `std::string` by value, not only is the code simpler, but there's also no need to write separate overloads for rvalue references.

The approach with passing by value is consistent with item 41 - "Consider pass by value for copyable parameters that are cheap to move and always copied" from Effective Modern C++ by Scott Meyers.

However, is `std::string` cheap to move?

Although the C++ Standard doesn't specify that, usually, strings are implemented with **Small String Optimisation (SSO)** - the string object contains extra space to fit characters without additional memory allocation³. That means that moving a string is the same as copying it. And since the string is short, the copy is also fast.

Let's reconsider our example of passing by value when the `string` is short:

```
UserName u1{"John"}; // fits in SSO buffer

std::string s2 {"Marc"}; // fits in SSO buffer
UserName u2 { s2 };

std::string s3 {"Marc"}; // fits in SSO buffer
UserName u3 { std::move(s3) };
```

Remember that each move is the same as a copy in a case of a short string.

For `const std::string&`:

- `u1` - two copies: one copy from the input string literal into a temporary string argument, then another copy into the member variable.
- `u2` - one copy: the existing string is bound to the reference argument, and then we have one copy into the member variable.
- `u3` - one copy: the `rvalue` reference is bound to the input parameter at no cost; later we have a copy into the member field.

For `std::string`:

- `u1` - two copies: the input argument is created from a string literal, and then there's a copy into `name_`.
- `u2` - two copies: one copy into the argument, and then there's the second copy into the member.
- `u3` - two copies: one copy into the argument (move means copy in this particular case), and then there's the second copy into the member.

As you see, short strings passing by value might be "slower" when you pass some existing string simply because you have two copies rather than one. On the other hand, the compiler

---

³SSO is not standardized and prone to change. MSVC (VS 2013 and above)/GCC (8.1 and above) - it's a buffer of 16 bytes, and the empty string has a size of 32 bytes. It means a space for 15 characters of the `char` type, or 7 for `wchar_t`. In Clang (6.0 and above when compiled with `-stdlib=libc++`) the buffer might contain space for 22 characters of `char` but might be only a few characters for `wchar_t`. The size of an empty string is only 24 bytes. For multiplatform code, it's not a good idea to assume optimizations based on SSO. Read more at this good article: https://shaharmike.com/cpp/std-string/.

might optimize the code better when it sees an object and not a reference. Moreover, short strings are cheap to copy, so the potential "slowdown" might not even be visible.

All in all, passing by value and then moving from a string argument is the preferred solution. You have simple code and better performance for larger strings.

As always, if your code needs maximum performance, then you have to measure all possible cases.

Other Types & Automation

The problem discussed in this section can also be extended to other copyable and movable types. If the move operation is cheap, passing by value might be better than by reference. You can also use automation, like Clang-Tidy, which can detect potential improvements. Clang Tidy has a separate rule for that use case; see clang-tidy - modernize-pass-by-value[4].

Here's the summary of string passing and initialization of a string member:

Input Parameter	`const string&`	`string` and `move`
`const char*`	2 allocations	1 allocation + move
`const char*` SSO	2 copies	2 copies
lvalue	1 allocation	1 allocation + 1 move
lvalue SSO	1 copy	2 copies
rvalue	1 allocation	2 moves
rvalue SSO	1 copy	2 copies

This part covered only the basic approach with string references and string copies. We could also extend this discussion and cover the `std::string_view` added in C++17. If you want a complete comparison, see this blog post "How to Initialize a String Member" @C++Stories[5].

---

[4]https://clang.llvm.org/extra/clang-tidy/checks/modernize-pass-by-value.html
[5]https://www.cppstories.com/2018/08/init-string-member/

Reducing extra copies through `emplace` and `in_place`

Since C++11, programmers got a new technique to initialize objects "in place". This approach avoids unnecessary temporary copies and works with non-movable/non-copyable types.

As an example, let's look at `std::optional` and `std::variant` from C++17 and ways to construct those types efficiently.

The first vocabulary type, `std::optional`, is a wrapper with an extra feature to indicate whether or not the object is present. You can create optional objects almost in the same way as the wrapped object:

Ex 13.2. Simplified `std::optional` introduction. Run @Compiler Explorer

```cpp
#include <iostream>
#include <optional>

int main() {
    std::optional<double> empty;
    std::optional<std::string> ostr{"Hello World"};
    std::optional<int> oi{10};

    // has_value()
    if (empty.has_value()) std::cout << *empty << '\n';
    else std::cout << "empty is empty\n";

    // operator bool
    if (ostr) std::cout << *ostr << '\n';
    else std::cout << "ostr is empty\n";

    // value_or()
    std::cout << oi.value_or(42) << '\n';
}
```

As you can see, there's no need to explicitly state the type of the objects like:

```cpp
std::optional<std::string> ostr{std::string{"Hello World"}};
std::optional<int> oi{int{10}};
```

This is because `std::optional` has a constructor that takes `U&&` (an rvalue reference to a type that converts to the type stored in the optional). In our case, it's recognized as `const char*`, and strings can be initialized from this.

But let's have a look at two interesting creation techniques with `std::in_place_t` and `emplace()`:

We have at least two points: default constructor and efficient construction.

Default construction

If you have a class with a default constructor, like:

```cpp
class UserName {
public:
    UserName() : mName("Default") { }
    // ...
private:
    std::string mName;
};
```

How would you create a `std::optional` object that contains `UserName{}`?

You can write:

```cpp
std::optional<UserName> u0;     // empty optional
std::optional<UserName> u1{};   // also empty!

// optional with default constructed object:
std::optional<UserName> u2{UserName{}};
```

That works, but it creates an additional temporary object. Here's the output if you run the above code (augmented with some logging):

```
UserName::UserName('Default')
UserName::UserName(move 'Default')    // move temp object
UserName::~UserName('')               // delete the temp object
UserName::~UserName('Default')
```

The code creates a temporary object and then moves it into the object stored in `std::optional`.

Here we can use a more efficient constructor - by leveraging `std::in_place_t`:

```
std::optional<UserName> opt{std::in_place};
```

Produces the output:

```
UserName::UserName('Default')
UserName::~UserName('Default')
```

The object stored in the optional is created in place, in the same way as you'd call `UserName{}`. No additional copy or move is needed.

You can play with those examples here @Compiler Explorer[6].

Non-copyable/movable types

As you saw in the example from the previous section, if you use a temporary object to initialize the contained value inside `std::optional`, then the compiler will have to use the move or copy construction. But what if your type doesn't allow that? For example, `std::mutex` is not movable or copyable. In that case, `std::in_place` is the only way to work with such types.

Constructors with many arguments

Another use case is a situation where your type has more arguments in a constructor. By default, `optional` can work with a single argument (rvalue ref), and efficiently pass it to the wrapped type. What if you'd like to initialize `std::complex(double, double)` or `std::vector`?

You can always create a temporary copy and then pass it in the construction:

---
[6]https://godbolt.org/z/Kb9dP941h

```cpp
// vector with 4 1's:
std::optional<std::vector<int>> opt{std::vector<int>{4, 1}};
// complex type:
std::optional<std::complex<double>> opt2{std::complex<double>{0, 1}};
```

Or use `in_place` and the version of the constructor that handles the variable argument list:

```cpp
template< class... Args >
constexpr explicit optional(std::in_place_t, Args&&... args );
```

Or `initializer_list`:

```cpp
template< class U, class... Args >
constexpr explicit optional(std::in_place_t,std::initializer_list<U> ilist,
                            Args&&... args );
```

For example:

```cpp
std::optional<std::vector<int>> opt{std::in_place_t, 4, 1};
std::optional<std::complex<double>> opt2{std::in_place_t, 0, 1};
```

The option with `in_place_t` is quite verbose but omits the creation of temporary objects.

The `emplace()` member function

If you want to change the stored value inside optional, then you can use the assignment operator or call `emplace()`.

Following the concepts introduced in C++11 (emplace methods for containers), you can efficiently create (and destroy the old value if needed) a new object.

`std::make_optional()`

You can also look at the `make_optional` factory function:

```cpp
auto opt = std::make_optional<UserName>();
auto opt = std::make_optional<std::vector<int>>(4, 1);
```

The above code Is as efficient as:

```cpp
std::optional<UserName> opt{std::in_place};
std::optional<std::vector<int>> opt{std::in_place_t, 4, 1};
```

`make_optional` implement in place construction equivalent to:

```cpp
return std::optional<T>(std::in_place, std::forward<Args>(args)...);
```

In `std::variant`

`std::variant` has two `in_place` helpers that you can use:

- `std::in_place_type` - used to specify which type you want to change/set in the variant
- `std::in_place_index` - used to specify which index you want to change/set. Types are numerated from 0. For example, in a variant `std::variant<int, float, std::string>`: `int` has an index 0, `float` has an index 1, and the string has an index of 2. The index is the same value as returned from the `variant::index` member function.

Fortunately, you don't always have to use the helpers to create a variant. It's smart enough to recognize if it can be constructed from the passed single parameter:

```cpp
// this constructs the second/float:
std::variant<int, float, std::string> intFloatString { 10.5f };
```

For `std::variant`, we need the helpers for at least two cases:

- ambiguity - to distinguish which type should be created where several could match
- efficient complex type creation (similar to optional)

Note: by default variant is initialized with the first type - assuming it has a default constructor. If the default constructor is unavailable, you'll get a compiler error. This is different from `std::optional`, which is initialized to an empty optional - as mentioned in the previous section.

Ambiguity

What if you have initialization like:

```cpp
std::variant<int, float> intFloat { 10.5 }; // conversion from double?
```

The value `10.5` could be converted to `int` or `float`, so the compiler will report a few pages of template errors... but basically, it cannot deduce what type should `double` be converted to.

But you can easily handle such an error by specifying which type you'd like to create:

```cpp
std::variant<int, float> intFloat { std::in_place_index<0>, 10.5 };
// or
std::variant<int, float> intFloat { std::in_place_type<int>, 10.5 };
```

Complex types

Similarly to `std::optional`, if you want to create objects that get several constructor arguments efficiently, use `std::in_place*`: For example:

```cpp
// initializer list passed into vector
std::variant<std::vector<int>, std::string> vecStr {
    std::in_place_index<0>, { 0, 1, 2, 3 }
};
```

The copy and swap idiom

The implementation of `DataPacket` from the second chapter contained two versions of the assignment operator:

```cpp
DataPacket& operator=(const DataPacket& other) { }
DataPacket& operator=(DataPacket&& other) noexcept {}
```

The code inside those functions contains a bit of code duplication, and what's more, it's not entirely safe. For example, if we change one data member, but the other change throws an exception, our object will be in an invalid state (partially assigned). To improve, we can try writing a single function:

```cpp
DataPacket& operator=(DataPacket other) noexcept {
    using std::swap;
    swap(data_, other.data_);
    swap(checkSum_, other.checkSum_);
    swap(serverId_, other.serverId_);
    std::cout << "Assignment for \"" << data_ << "\"\n";
    return *this;
}
```

The first striking thing to notice is that the operator takes `DataPacket` by value. Before the operator's body, a fully initialized `DataPacket` object must be passed. In other words, the compiler will call a copy or move constructor for that purpose. Later we can use `swap` to exchange data members. I also wrote `using std::swap` so that the overload resolution can find all related `swap` functions, including those from the `std` namespace. `swap` cannot throw exceptions (as those functions are usually marked with `noexcept`) our assignment operator is safe and won't cause "partially assigned"/invalid objects. Additionally, since we have an object created in the input argument, there's no need to check against `== this`. Let's invoke the new assignment implementation:

```cpp
DataPacket another { ... };
DataPacket newOne { ... };
another = newOne;
```

In the above use case, the compiler creates a copy of `newOne` and passes it as the `another` argument in the assignment operator.

On the other hand, below, you can see a case where a move constructor will be called to create the `other` argument before it's passed to the assignment operator:

```cpp
DataPacket another { ... };
DataPacket newOne { ... };
another = std::move(newCar);
```

You can play with this example @Compiler Explorer[7].

To fully implement the idiom, we could add a `DataPacket::swap` function that could be reused in the copy and the move constructor. For example:

---

[7]https://godbolt.org/z/esoqY97cx

```cpp
DataPacket(DataPacket&& other) noexcept
: DataPacket() { // make sure data is initialized
    swap(*this, other);
    std::cout << "Move ctor for \"" << data_ << "\"\n";
}
DataPacket& operator=(DataPacket other) noexcept {
    swap(*this, other);
    std::cout << "Assignment for \"" << data_ << "\"\n";
    return *this;
}

friend void swap(DataPacket& a, DataPacket& b) noexcept {
    using std::swap;
    swap(a.data_, b.data_);
    swap(a.checkSum_, b.checkSum_);
    swap(a.serverId_, b.serverId_);
}
```

See this alternative version @Compiler Explorer[8].

The move constructor version only works if the member variables are correctly initialized when defined (that's why we have to call a default constructor or use NSDMI described in another chapter). If you use swap with a move constructor and the variables haven't been initialized, then the swap will swap with indeterminate values!

The idea for the idiom is intensely discussed in this Stack Overflow Question: c++ - What is the copy-and-swap idiom?[9].

CRTP class counter

In the chapter about `inline` variables, there was an example called "Instance Counter". It is a handy type that could be used to count instances of other types separately. For example, we could inherit from it to share the code. Unfortunately, there's an issue with such a simple approach:

---

[8]https://godbolt.org/z/Me5189Wr8
[9]https://stackoverflow.com/questions/3279543/what-is-the-copy-and-swap-idiom

Ex 13.3. The **InstanceCounter** type. Run @Compiler Explorer

```cpp
class InstanceCounter {
    static inline size_t counter_ { 0 };
public:
    InstanceCounter() noexcept { ++counter_; }
    InstanceCounter(const InstanceCounter& ) noexcept { ++counter_; }
    InstanceCounter(InstanceCounter&& ) noexcept { ++counter_; }
    ~InstanceCounter() noexcept { --counter_; }
    static size_t GetInstanceCounter() { return counter_; }
};

struct Value : InstanceCounter {
    int val { 0 };
};
struct Wrapper : InstanceCounter {
    double val { 0.0 };
};

int main() {
    Value v;
    Wrapper w;
    std::cout << "Values: " << Value::GetInstanceCounter() << '\n';
    std::cout << "Wrappers: " << Wrapper::GetInstanceCounter() << '\n';
}
```

If you run this code, you'll see the following output:

```
Values: 2
Wrappers: 2
```

The main trouble is that both classes share the single base class, and thus there's only one "copy" of the `counter_` static data member. We want to count the objects separately and therefore need to have distinct counters. To fix the problem, we can use a technique called *Curiously Recurring Template Pattern* (CRTP).

The core idea is to have a class that derives from a class template using itself as a template parameter.

```
template<class Derived>
class Base {};
class X : public Base<X> {};
```

Now, each derived class will have a separate "copy" of the `Base` class, which opens at least two possibilities:

- Add common functionality to derived classes and improves their interface.
- A way to implement static polymorphism. The base class might implement a member function that accesses the Derived class and calls the Derived implementation.

We can implement our counter helper in the following way:

Ex 13.4. The `InstanceCounter` CRTP version. Run @Compiler Explorer

```
template <typename Derived>
class InstanceCounter {
    static inline size_t counter_ { 0 };
public:
    InstanceCounter() noexcept { ++counter_; }
    InstanceCounter(const InstanceCounter& ) noexcept { ++counter_; }
    InstanceCounter(InstanceCounter&& ) noexcept { ++counter_; }
    ~InstanceCounter() noexcept { --counter_; }

    static size_t GetInstanceCounter() { return counter_; }
};

struct Value : InstanceCounter<Value> {
    int val { 0 };
};
struct Wrapper : InstanceCounter<Wrapper> {
    double val { 0.0 };
};

int main() {
    Value v;
    Wrapper w;
    std::cout << "Values: " << Value::GetInstanceCounter() << '\n';
    std::cout << "Wrappers: " << Wrapper::GetInstanceCounter() << '\n';
}
```

Now the output is:

```
Values: 1
Wrappers: 1
```

As you can see, we created two different template instantiations for InstanceCounter. There's one for Value and the second for Wrapper. Now the counters are separate and show the expected values.

 Read more about this handy technique in Curiously Recurring Template Pattern @C++Reference[10] and also in a three-part series at the Fluent C++ blog: The Curiously Recurring Template Pattern (CRTP), part 1[11].

Several initialization types in one class

As the demo of various initialization techniques, I'd like to show code that creates N random "application windows."

Here are the core points of the demo:

- A Window class contains basic parameters like name (on the title bar), width, height, and some flags (bits per pixel, visibility).
- The demo selects a random number X and will try to generate X Window objects.
- Each object will have a random name composed of predefined words and a random size.
- The application prints each window using std::cout.
- As an additional check, an InstanceCounter class counts the number of Window objects. We can use this helper to verify the correctness of the demo.

Here's the first part that defines the Flags object:

---

[10] https://en.cppreference.com/w/cpp/language/crtp
[11] https://www.fluentcpp.com/2017/05/12/curiously-recurring-template-pattern/

Ex 13.5. The Flags type. Run @Compiler Explorer

```cpp
struct Flags {
    unsigned bppMode_ : 4 { 0 }; // bits per pixel
    unsigned visible_ : 1 { 1 };
    unsigned extData  : 2 { 0 };
};
```

Here's the main class:

Ex 13.5. The Window type. Run @Compiler Explorer

```cpp
class Window : public InstanceCounter<Window> {
    static constexpr unsigned default_width  { 1028 };
    static constexpr unsigned default_height { 768 };
    static constexpr unsigned default_bpp    { 8 };

    unsigned width_  { default_width };
    unsigned height_ { default_height };
    Flags flags_ {.bppMode_ { default_bpp } };
    std::string title_ { "Default Window" };

public:
    Window() = default;
    explicit Window(std::string title) : title_(std::move(title)) { }
    Window(std::string title, unsigned w, unsigned h) :
    width_(w), height_(h), title_(std::move(title)) {}

    friend std::ostream& operator<<(std::ostream& os, const Window& w) {
        os << w.title_ << ": " << w.width_ << "x" << w.height_;
        return os;
    }
};
```

The Window class uses several features discussed in the book:

- NSDMI to initialize data members,
- designated initializers from C++20, combined with NSDMI for the flags_ data member,

- Custom constructors that offer several options to initialize the data members,
- We inherit from `InstanceCounter`, so each constructor invocation for the `Window` will also invoke the appropriate constructor in `InstanceCounter`. Similarly, the `InstanceCounter` destructor will be nicely called from the implicit default destructor of the `Window` class.

And now the final demo code:

Ex 13.5. The Window type. Run @Compiler Explorer

```cpp
void WindowDemo() {
    std::random_device rd;
    std::mt19937 gen(rd());
    std::uniform_int_distribution<> distrib(0, 20);

    const int windowCount = std::uniform_int_distribution<>(2, 10)(gen);
    std::cout << "Generating " << windowCount << " random Windows\n";

    const std::array adjs { "regular ", "empty ", "blue ", "super " };
    const std::array nouns { "app", "tool", "console", "game" };
    const std::array sizes { 1080u, 1920u, 768u, 320u, 640u, 3840u, 800u };

    std::vector<Window> windows;
    for (int i = 0; i < windowCount; ++i) {
        auto r = distrib(gen);
        auto r2 = distrib(gen);
        auto name = std::string { adjs[(r + i) % adjs.size()] } +
                    nouns[r2 % nouns.size()];
        Window w{name, sizes[r2 % sizes.size()],
                 sizes[r % sizes.size()]};
        windows.push_back(w);
    }

    for (const auto& w : windows)
        std::cout << w << '\n';

    std::cout << "Created " << Window::GetInstanceCounter() << " Windows\n";
}

int main() {
```

```
        WindowDemo();

        if (Window::GetInstanceCounter() != 0) {
            std::cout << Window::GetInstanceCounter()
                      << " Windows are still alive!\n";
        }
}
```

Here's the possible output:

```
Generating 8 random Windows
super tool: 320x320
regular tool: 320x640
super game: 1080x768
super game: 640x1080
regular tool: 1920x3840
empty tool: 1920x3840
blue game: 320x768
empty console: 320x320
Created 8 Windows
```

In `WindowDemo`, the code declares some basic data and generates a random number. Later, in the main loop, we generate random numbers to pick values from `adjs`, `nouns`, and `sizes` arrays. Once the data is ready, I can create a `Window` object and place it in the `std::vector`. To show the creation of the `Window` object, I used `push_back` on a vector, but we can optimize it and call `emplace_back`, which doesn't need a temporary object:

```
windows.emplace_back(name, sizes[r2%sizes.size()], sizes[r%sizes.size()]);
```

Later there's another loop that prints all windows.

 In the code, I didn't have to specify the full type for `std::array<Type, Count>` as the compiler could deduce everything for me! Thanks to Class Type Argument Deduction (CTAD) and Deduction guides from C++17, the compiler can help us save some typing. See more @C++Reference - deduction guides for array[12].

---

[12]https://en.cppreference.com/w/cpp/container/array/deduction_guides

The code uses `InstanceCounter` as a bonus debugging facility to ensure we have the correct number of active objects. When `WindowDemo()` finishes, all instances should be removed, and we can double-check it inside `main()`.

Meyers Singleton and C++11

Meyers Singleton is a design pattern in C++ that is used to ensure that a class has only one instance and provides a global access point to that instance. The pattern is named after Scott Meyers, who described it in his book "Effective C++: 55 Specific Ways to Improve Your Programs and Designs".

To implement Meyers Singleton in C++, you can define a class with a private default constructor, a private copy constructor, and a private assignment operator. You can then provide a public `static` function that returns a reference to the single instance of the class. The first time this function is called, it creates a new instance of the class and returns a reference to it. Subsequent calls to the function return a reference to the same instance. Here is an example:

Ex 13.6. Basic Meyers singleton. Run @Compiler Explorer

```cpp
#include <cstdio>
class Singleton {
private:
  Singleton() { puts("Singleton()"); }
  Singleton(const Singleton&) = delete;
  Singleton& operator=(const Singleton&) = delete;

public:
  static Singleton& getInstance() {
    static Singleton instance;
    return instance;
  }

  void foo() { puts("foo()"); }
  void func() { puts("func()"); }
};

int main() {
    puts("main starts...");
```

```
    Singleton::getInstance().foo();
    Singleton::getInstance().func();
}
```

When we run the code, we'll get the following output:

```
main starts...
Singleton()
foo()
func()
```

As you can see in the output, we called `getInstance()` two times, but the real instance was created only once (the constructor was called once).

Meyers Singleton is often used to ensure that a class has only one instance and provides a global access point to that instance. In C++11 and later, it is possible to use the `static` keyword to declare a local `static` variable within a function. This allows you to define a local variable that is initialized only once in a thread-safe way.

 While Meyers Singleton is a very efficient way to implement this design pattern, singletons don't have a good opinion in modern programming style. A singleton, in fact, is a global object, leading to a few problems like testing, scalability, lack of explicit dependencies, and others. Please be careful when adding this pattern to your code.

Factory with self-registering types and static initialization

Let's have a look at a typical factory function below. It creates `ZipCompression` or `BZCompression` based on the extensions of the filename.

```
static unique_ptr<ICompressionMethod> Create(const string& fileName) {
    auto extension = GetExtension(filename);
    if (extension == "zip")
        return make_unique<ZipCompression>();
    else if (extension = "bz")
        return make_unique<BZCompression>();

    return nullptr;
}
```

Here are some issues with this approach:

- Each time you write a new class, and you want to include it in the factory, you have to add another if in the `Create()` method. Easy to forget in a complex system.
- All the types must be known to the factory.
- In `Create()`, we arbitrarily used strings to represent types. Such representation is only visible in that single method. What if you'd like to use it somewhere else? Strings might be easily misspelled, especially if you have several places where they are compared.

All in all, we get a strong dependency between the factory and the classes.

But what if classes could register themselves? Would that help?

- The factory would do its job: create new objects based on some matching.
- If you write a new class, there's no need to change parts of the factory class. Such a class would register automatically.

To give you more motivation, I'd like to show one real-life example. When you use Google Test library, and you write:

```
TEST(MyModule, InitTest) {
    // impl...
}
```

Behind this single `TEST` macro, a lot of things happen! For starters, your test is expanded into a separate class - so each test is a new class. But then, there's a problem: you have all the tests, so how the test runner knows about them? It's the same problem were' trying to solve in this section. The classes need to be auto-registered.

Have a look at this code: from googletest/.../gtest-internal.h[13]:

---

[13] https://github.com/google/googletest/blob/ea31cb15f0c2ab9f5f5b18e82311eb522989d747/googletest/include/gtest/internal/gtest-internal.h#L1218

```
// (some parts of the code cut out)
#define GTEST_TEST_(test_case_name, test_name, parent_class, parent_id)\
class GTEST_TEST_CLASS_NAME_(test_case_name, test_name) \
 : public parent_class { \
  virtual void TestBody();\
  static ::testing::TestInfo* const test_info_ GTEST_ATTRIBUTE_UNUSED_;\
};\
\
::testing::TestInfo* const GTEST_TEST_CLASS_NAME_(test_case_name, test_name)\
  ::test_info_ =\
    ::testing::internal::MakeAndRegisterTestInfo(\
        #test_case_name, #test_name, NULL, NULL, \
        new ::testing::internal::TestFactoryImpl<\
            GTEST_TEST_CLASS_NAME_(test_case_name, test_name)>);\
void GTEST_TEST_CLASS_NAME_(test_case_name, test_name)::TestBody()
```

I cut some parts of the code to make it shorter, but basically, `GTEST_TEST_` is used in the `TEST` macro, and this will expand to a new class. In the lower section, you might see the name `MakeAndRegisterTestInfo`. So here's the place where the class registers!

After the registration, the runner knows all the existing tests and can invoke them.

Here are the steps to implement a similar system:

- Some Interface - we'd like to create classes derived from one interface. It's the exact requirement as a "normal" factory method.
- Factory class that also holds a map of available types.
- A proxy that will be used to create a given class. The factory doesn't know how to create a given type now, so we have to provide some proxy classes.

For the interface, we can use `ICompressionMethod`:

```cpp
class ICompressionMethod {
public:
    ICompressionMethod() = default;
    virtual ~ICompressionMethod() = default;
    virtual void Compress() = 0;
};
```

And then the factory:

```cpp
class CompressionMethodFactory {
public:
    using TCreateMethod = unique_ptr<ICompressionMethod>(*)();
public:
    CompressionMethodFactory() = delete;

    static bool Register(const string& name, TCreateMethod funcCreate);
    static unique_ptr<ICompressionMethod> Create(const string& name);
private:
    static Map<string, TCreateMethod> s_methods;
};
```

The factory holds the map of registered types. The main point is that the factory now uses some method (TCreateMethod) to create the desired type (our proxy). The name of a type and that creation method must be initialized in a different place.

The implementation of the factory:

```cpp
class CompressionMethodFactory {
public:
    using TCreateMethod = unique_ptr<ICompressionMethod>(*)();
public:
    CompressionMethodFactory() = delete;

    static constexpr bool Register(string_view name,
                                   TCreateMethod createFunc) {
        if (auto val = s_methods.at(name, nullptr); val == nullptr) {
            if (s_methods.insert(name, createFunc)) {
                std::cout << name << " registered\n";
                return true;
            }
        }
        return false;
    }
    static std::unique_ptr<ICompressionMethod> Create(string_view name) {
        if (auto val = s_methods.at(name, nullptr); val != nullptr) {
            std::cout << "calling " << name << "\n";
            return val();
        }
```

```
        return nullptr;
    }
private:
    static inline constinit Map<string_view, TCreateMethod, 4> s_methods;
};
```

Now we can implement a derived class from `ICompressionMethod` that will register in the factory:

```
class ZipCompression : public ICompressionMethod {
public:
    virtual void Compress() override;

    static unique_ptr<ICompressionMethod> CreateMethod() {
        return std::make_unique<ZipCompression>();
    }
    static string_view GetFactoryName() { return "ZIP"; }
private:
    static inline bool s_registered =
    CompressionMethodFactory::Register(ZipCompression::GetFactoryName(),
                                       CreateMethod);
};
```

The downside of self-registration is that there's a bit more work for a class. As you can see, we must have a static `CreateMethod` defined.

To register such a class, all we have to do is to define `s_registered`:

```
bool ZipCompression::s_registered =
  CompressionMethodFactory::Register(ZipCompression::GetFactoryName(),
                                     ZipCompression::CreateMethod);
```

The basic idea for this mechanism is that we rely on static variables. They will be initialized before `main()` is called.

Because the order of initialization of static variables in different compilation units is unspecified, we might end up with a different order of elements in the factory container. Each name/type is not dependent on other already registered types in our example, so we're safe here.

But what about the first insertion? Can we be sure that the Map is created and ready for use?

That's why I implemented a special version of Map which has a constexpr constructor (implicit) and, thanks to constinit, will be initialized before s_registered is initialized (for some first registered class).

 My current implementation uses std::array, which can be used in constant expressions and doesn't require dynamic memory allocations. Alternatively, you can also use a static variable returned from a function (similar to Meyers Singleton), and this will also guarantee proper initialization order. Note that using std::vector for the map implementation won't work in C++20. std::vector can be used at compile-time, but memory allocations from compile-time are not transient.

We should also ask one question: Can the compiler eliminate s_registered? Fortunately, we're also on the safe side. From the latest draft of C++: [basic.stc.static#2][14]:

> If a variable with static storage duration has initialization or a destructor with side effects, it shall not be eliminated even if it appears to be unused, except that a class object or its copy/move may be eliminated as specified in class.copy.elision.

Since s_registered has an initialization with side effects (calling Register()), the compiler cannot optimize it.

See the full example:

Ex 13.7. Factory and Self-registering classes demo. Run @Wandbox

```
#include "ICompressionMethod.h"
#include "ZipCompression.h"
#include <iostream>

int main() {
    std::cout << "main starts...\n";
    if (auto pMethod = CompressionMethodFactory::Create("ZIP"); pMethod)
        pMethod->Compress();
    else
```

---

[14] https://timsong-cpp.github.io/cppwp/basic.stc.static#2

```cpp
        std::cout << "Cannot find ZIP...\n";
    
    if (auto pMethod = CompressionMethodFactory::Create("BZ"); pMethod)
        pMethod->Compress();
    else
        std::cout << "Cannot find BZ...\n";
    
    if (auto pMethod = CompressionMethodFactory::Create("7Z"); pMethod)
        pMethod->Compress();
    else
        std::cout << "Cannot find 7Z...\n";
}
```

You can find more about this technique, including a topic about static libraries in two articles at C++ Stories: Solving Undefined Behavior in Factories with constinit from C++20 @C++ Stories[15] and Static Variables Initialization in a Static Library, Example @C++ Stories[16].

Summary

It was a fun ride! And I hope you enjoyed the techniques that we discussed in this chapter. We went from passing string types, reducing extra copies through in_place, to Copy And Swap, CRTP, and even self-registering types. The main goal was not only to experiment with artificial examples but to show some practical techniques where the knowledge of C++ initialization details is helpful.

---

[15] https://www.cppstories.com/2023/ub-factory-constinit/
[16] https://www.cppstories.com/2018/02/static-vars-static-lib/

14. The Final Quiz And Exercises

Congratulations on completing the whole book! Now you can check your knowledge and try answering a few quiz questions and solving exercises.

Each question has only one correct answer.

1. Which C++ Standard did add in-class default member initializers?

1. C++98
2. C++11
3. C++14
4. C++17

2. Can you use `auto` type deduction for non-static data members?

1. Yes, since C++11
2. No
3. Yes, since C++20

3. Do you need to define a `static inline` data member in a cpp file?

1. No, the definition happens at the same place where a static inline member is declared.
2. Yes, the compiler needs the definition in a cpp file.
3. Yes, the compiler needs a definition in all translation units that use this variable.

4. Can a `static inline` variable be non-constant?

1. Yes, it's just a regular variable.
2. No, inline variables must be constant.

5. What's the output of the following code:

```
struct S {
    int a { 10 };
    int b { 42 };
};
S s { 1 };
std::cout << s.a << ", " << s.b;
```

1. 1, 0
2. 10, 42
3. 1, 42

6. Consider the following code:

```
struct C {
    C(int x) : a(x) { }
    int a { 10 };
    int b { 42 };
};
C c(0);
```

Select the `true` statement:

1. `C::a` is initialized twice. The first time, it's initialized with `10` and then the second time with `0` in the constructor.
2. `C::a` is initialized only once with `0` in the constructor.
3. The code doesn't compile because the compiler cannot decide how to initialize the `C::a` member.

7. What happens when you throw an exception from a constructor?

1. The object is considered "created" so it will follow the regular lifetime of an object.
2. The object is considered "partially created," and thus, the compiler won't call its destructor.
3. The compiler calls `std::terminate` as you cannot throw exceptions from constructors.

8. What happens when you compile this code?

```
struct Point { int x; int y; };
Point pt {.y = 10, .x = 11 };
std::cout << pt.x << ", " << pt.y;
```

Select the `true` statement:

1. The code doesn't compile. Designators have to be in the same order as the data members in the `Point` class.
2. The code compiles and prints 11, 10.
3. The code compiles and prints 10, 11.

9. Will this code work in C++11?

```
struct User { std::string name = "unknown"; unsigned age { 0 }; };
User u { "John", 101 };
```

1. Yes, the code compiles in C++11 mode.
2. The code compiles starting with C++14 mode.
3. The code doesn't compile even in C++20.

10. Does the following struct have a compiler-generated copy constructor?

```
struct Test {
   Test() = default;
   Test(Test&& t) { /* some implementation*/ }
   int val { 10 };
};
```

1. Yes, it's a simple class type so copy constructor will be implicitly defined.
2. No, the class declares a user-defined move constructor, which prevents implicit copy constructor.
3. No, the class declares a default constructor, which prevents an implicit copy constructor.

11. Assume you have a `std::map<string, int> m;`. Select the single true statement about the following loop:

```
for (const pair<string, int>& elem : m)
```

1. The loop properly iterates over the map, creating no extra copies.
2. The loop will create a copy of each element in the map as the type of `elem` mismatches.
3. The code won't compile as a `const pair` cannot bind to a map.

12. According to C++20, is `auto x { 42 };` same as `auto z = { 42 };`?

1. Yes, x and z will have the same type - `int`.
2. Yes, x and z will have the same type - `int &&`.
3. No, x will be `int`, but z is `initializer_list<int>`.

13. Consider the following code and select true statements:

```
std::optional<std::complex<double>> opt1{std::complex<double>{0, 1}};
std::optional<std::complex<double>> opt2{std::in_place_t, 0, 1};
```

1. `opt1` is initialized less efficiently, as we have to create a temporary object, `opt2` doesn't use any temporary objects.
2. `opt1` is initialized as efficiently as `opt2`; no extra copies are created.
3. you cannot use `in_place_t` in the `std::optional` creation.

14. Is Meyers singleton safe in C++03? Select the best matching statement.

1. Yes, it uses a static variable in a function scope, so the compiler will make sure it's initialized before the first use.
2. Yes, C++03 ensures both thread safety and one-time initialization.
3. No, only C++11 introduced thread safety for static local variables, so this singleton pattern is only safe from C++11.

15. Does the following statement compile?

```
std::vector<std::unique_ptr<int>> ints {
    std::make_unique<int>(1), std::make_unique<int>(2)
};
```

1. No, it doesn't compile, as we have an `initializer_list` of non-copyable types (`unique_ptr`) and `initializer_list` requires a copy.
2. Yes, it compiles, as `initializer_list` handles non-copyable types.
3. Yes, it compiles because compilers can elide those extra copies.

Please write down your answers and check them in Appendix B.

Exercises

Check your skills with four coding exercises.

For the print book, you can download the starting code in the "chapter 14 - exercises" folder. There's a link to an online compiler at the top of each file.

See https://github.com/fenbf/cppinitbook_public/tree/main/examples.

Exercise 1: NSDMI

Below is the `Point` class declaration with two data members.

```
struct Point {
    double x;
    double y;
};
```

Update this class so that it uses NSDMI and initializes `Point::x` to `1.0` and `Point::y` to `2.0`.

Here's the code for test cases:

```
TEST(PointTest, X) {
    Point p;
    EXPECT_DOUBLE_EQ(1.0, p.x);
}

TEST(PointTest, Y) {
    Point p;
    EXPECT_DOUBLE_EQ(2.0, p.y);
}
```

You can practice with the following Compiler Explorer solution: Point tests @Compiler Explorer[1].

When you run the code, you'll see that the test failed:

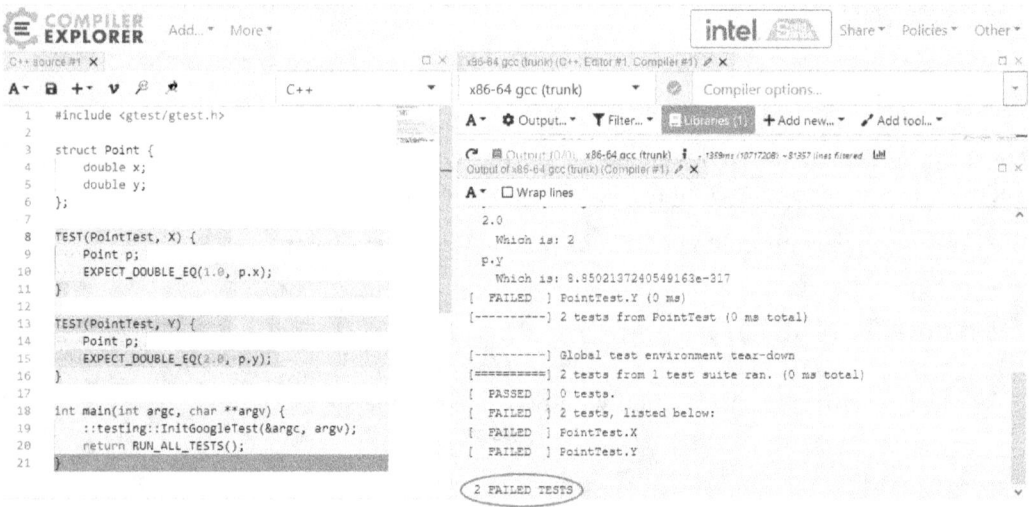

Your task is to improve the code so that tests pass:

---

[1] https://godbolt.org/z/Gor1Y8qx7

```
 8   TEST(PointTest, X) {
 9       Point p;
10       EXPECT_DOUBLE_EQ(1.0, p.x);
11   }
12
13   TEST(PointTest, Y) {
14       Point p;
15       EXPECT_DOUBLE_EQ(2.0, p.y);
16   }
17
18   int main(int argc, char **argv) {
19       ::testing::InitGoogleTest(&argc, argv);
20       return RUN_ALL_TESTS();
21   }
```

```
ASM generation compiler returned: 0
Execution build compiler returned: 0
Program returned: 0
[==========] Running 2 tests from 1 test suite.
[----------] Global test environment set-up.
[----------] 2 tests from PointTest
[ RUN      ] PointTest.X
[       OK ] PointTest.X (0 ms)
[ RUN      ] PointTest.Y
[       OK ] PointTest.Y (0 ms)
[----------] 2 tests from PointTest (0 ms total)

[----------] Global test environment tear-down
[==========] 2 tests from 1 test suite ran. (0 ms total)
[  PASSED  ] 2 tests.
```

Exercise 2: NSDMI

Let's try another use case. Below, there's a structure called `SalesRecord`.

```cpp
#include <string>

constexpr unsigned int DEFAULT_CATEGORY = 4;
constexpr unsigned int DEFAULT_FLAGS = 0x0a;

struct SalesRecord {
    std::string name_;
    double price_;
    unsigned int category_ : 4;
    unsigned flags_ : 4;
};
```

Use NSDMI to initialize the data members to the following values:

- `name_` should be `"empty"`
- `price_` should be `1.0`
- `category_` should be `DEFAULT_CATEGORY`
- `flags_` should be `DEFAULT_FLAGS`

Here's the code for the test to solve:

```
TEST(SalesRecord, Name) {
    SalesRecord s;
    EXPECT_EQ("empty", s.name_);
}

TEST(SalesRecord, Price) {
    SalesRecord s;
    EXPECT_DOUBLE_EQ(1.0, s.price_);
}

TEST(SalesRecord, Category) {
    SalesRecord s;
    EXPECT_EQ(DEFAULT_CATEGORY, s.category_);
}

TEST(SalesRecord, Flags) {
    SalesRecord s;
    EXPECT_EQ(DEFAULT_FLAGS, s.flags_);
}
```

You can practice with the following Compiler Explorer solution: Point tests @Compiler Explorer[2].

Exercise 3: inline variables

We can combine our knowledge about constructors and inline variables and continue with the CountedType introduced in the Non-local types chapter. Please implement the support for other constructors so that the following test passes.

```
struct CountedType {
    static inline int instanceCounter = 0;
    static inline int maxInstanceCounter = 0;

    // your code here...
};
```

And here are the test cases:

---

[2] https://godbolt.org/z/Y19jMs4Gb

```cpp
int main() {
    {
        CountedType c0;
        CountedType c1;
        Tests::Expect(2, CountedType::instanceCounter);
        Tests::Expect(2, CountedType::maxInstanceCounter);

        CountedType c2(c1);
        CountedType c3(c1);
        Tests::Expect(4, CountedType::instanceCounter);
        Tests::Expect(4, CountedType::maxInstanceCounter);

        CountedType c4(std::move(c1));
        Tests::Expect(5, CountedType::instanceCounter);
        Tests::Expect(5, CountedType::maxInstanceCounter);
    }
    Tests::Expect(0, CountedType::instanceCounter);
    Tests::Expect(5, CountedType::maxInstanceCounter);
}
```

As you can see, the example creates several CountedType instances and then checks (via Test::Expect) if the counters are correct.

Start from the following runnable code sample @Wandbox[3], Click "Clone & Edit" to start the example, and make changes.

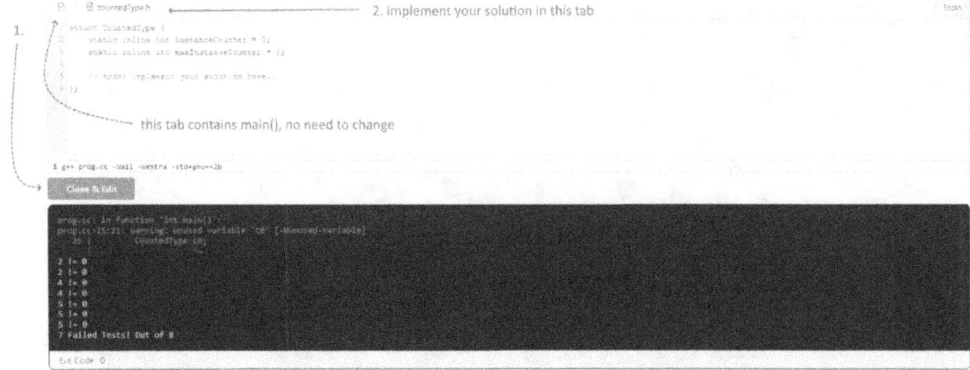

The starting point for the exercise, Click "Clone & Edit" to start the example

---

[3]https://wandbox.org/permlink/GuGzTWKF8irN2YLz

Exercise 4: Fix the code

Look at the code below and fix issues in `SalesRec`, `addPromo`, and `computeTotal` that make tests fail.

```cpp
struct SalesRec { std::string name_;  double price_; };

void addPromo(std::vector<SalesRec>& sales, double discount) {
    for (auto elem : sales)
        elem.price_ = (1.0-discount)*elem.price_;
}

double computeTotal(const std::vector<SalesRec>& sales) {
    double sum;
    for (auto elem : sales)
        sum += elem.price_;
    return sum;
}

TEST(computeTotal, empty) { ... }      // fails...
TEST(computeTotal, several) { ... }    // fails...
TEST(addPromo, simple) { ... }         // fails...
TEST(addPromo, two) { ... }            // fails...
```

Here's the starting code example @Compiler Explorer[4].

---
[4]https://godbolt.org/z/54dh8eh3h

Appendix A - Rules for Special Member Function Generation

In the chapters about constructors and destructor, we discussed when a compiler implicitly generates a given special member for a class type. In this appendix, you'll see a handy summary of the rules and guidelines for most common use cases.

The diagram

A C++ expert Howard Hinnant, a few years ago created a diagram[5] with the rules:

	Default constructor	Destructor	Copy constructor	Copy assignment	Move constructor	Move assignment
Nothing	defaulted	defaulted	defaulted	defaulted	defaulted	defaulted
Any constructor	not declared	defaulted	defaulted	defaulted	defaulted	defaulted
Default constructor	user declared	defaulted	defaulted	defaulted	defaulted	defaulted
Destructor	defaulted	user declared	defaulted*	defaulted*	not declared	not declared
Copy constructor	not declared	defaulted	user declared	defaulted*	not declared	not declared
Copy assignment	defaulted	defaulted	defaulted*	user declared	not declared	not declared
Move constructor	not declared	defaulted	deleted	deleted	user declared	not declared
Move assignment	defaulted	defaulted	deleted	deleted	not declared	user declared

---

[5] diagram redrawn, with permission of Howard Hinnant.

Howard is a lead designer and author of the C++11 proposal for move semantics, the `std::chrono` library, and a few other vital parts of Modern C++. The diagram, along with an informative description, can be found on this page: C++ class declarations[6] and also see this presentation: Everything you need to know about move semantics - Howard Hinnant @YouTube[7].

How to read the diagram:

Labels:

- defaulted - compiler generates the function if possible.
- defaulted* - deprecated behavior since C++11; the compiler might warn about a function generation.
- not-declared - there's no declaration of a function, so it won't participate in the overload resolution.
- deleted - the function is `=delete`, meaning that it participates in the overload resolution, but it won't be accessible.
- user declared - a given function is declared by the user and not implicitly provided by the compiler. That includes empty implementation, `=default`, or even `=delete`.

Rules:

- If a user declares no special member functions, the compiler defaults all special member functions.
- If a user declares any constructor, the compiler defaults all special member functions except for the default constructor
- If a user declares a default constructor, the compiler defaults all special member functions.
- If a user declares a destructor, the compiler defaults a default constructor, copy constructor and copy assignment operations. The move constructor and move assignment are not declared. The approach is deprecated, and compilers might warn about such behavior. When you declare a destructor, there's a high chance the default copy constructor might be insufficient.
- If a user declares a copy constructor, the compiler doesn't declare the default constructor, destructor, and copy assignment is defaulted. The move constructor and move assignment are not declared.

---

[6]https://howardhinnant.github.io/classdecl.html
[7]https://www.youtube.com/watch?v=vLinb2fgkHk

- If a user declares a copy assignment, the compiler default constructor, destructor, and copy assignment are defaulted. The move constructor and move assignment are not declared.
- If a user declares a move constructor, the compiler doesn't declare the default constructor, and the destructor is defaulted. The move assignment is not declared. The most important part is that the copy constructor and the copy assignment operator are deleted.
- If a user declares a move assignment, the compiler defaults a default constructor and destructor. The move constructor is not declared. The copy constructor and the copy assignment operator are deleted.

More functions provided

In a row, there's only one "user-declared" function, but if your class type has more than one special member function declared, then you have to look at the intersection of the matching rows. For example, suppose you declare a default constructor and a move assignment. In that case, the compiler will provide a default implementation for the destructor but will delete copy operations and not declare the move constructor.

Inheritance

And how about base and derived classes?

- A default constructor for a class T will be defined as deleted if T has a direct or virtual base that has a deleted default constructor, or it is ambiguous or inaccessible from this constructor.
- A copy constructor for a class T will be defined as deleted if T has a direct or virtual base class that cannot be copied (has deleted, inaccessible, or ambiguous copy constructors).
- A move constructor for a class T will be defined as deleted if T has a direct or virtual base class that cannot be moved (has deleted, inaccessible, or ambiguous move constructors).

For example:

```
struct Base { Base(Base&&) = delete; };
struct Derived : Base { };

int main() {
    Derived d; // won't compile!
}
```

The above code doesn't compile. We delete the move constructor from the `Base` class. This means that the move constructor in the `Derived` type is also deleted. In both types, the default constructor is not declared and not accessible.

Rule of zero

In most cases, defining a `class` without any special member functions will work:

```
struct RuleOfZero {
    // no custom special member functions...
    // member functions...
    // data members...
};
```

In the above case, the `RuleOfZero` class has all special member functions implicitly defined by the compiler.

See the following rule from the C++ Coding Guideline: C.20: If you can avoid defining default operations, do[8].

Rule of three (deprecated!)

Before C++11 (no move semantics), you could implement all special member functions:

---

[8]https://isocpp.github.io/CppCoreGuidelines/CppCoreGuidelines#c20-if-you-can-avoid-defining-default-operations-do

```
struct OldRuleOfThree {
    ~OldRuleOfThree();
    OldRuleOfThree(const OldRuleOfThree& other);
    OldRuleOfThree& operator=(const OldRuleOfThree& other);
};
```

However, since C++11, you **shouldn't use this pattern**, as having a copy operation declared won't declare the move operations. The lack of move operations will "slow down" the code that uses those objects, as the compiler will use copy operations rather than optimize with move.

Rule of 5 and 6 - modern C++

Suppose you implement a class that serves as a container or a manager for a resource. In that case, you probably need to implement all special member functions (in this version, RuleOfFive uses the Copy And Swap approach[9]).

```
struct RuleOfFive {
    RuleOfFive();
    ~RuleOfFive() noexcept;
    RuleOfFive(const RuleOfFive& other);
    RuleOfFive(RuleOfFive&& other) noexcept;
    RuleOfFive& operator=(RuleOfFive other) noexcept;
};


struct RuleOfSix {
    RuleOfSix();
    ~RuleOfSix() noexcept;
    RuleOfSix(const RuleOfSix& other);
    RuleOfSix& operator=(const RuleOfSix& other);
    RuleOfSix(RuleOfSix&& other) noexcept;
    RuleOfSix& operator=(RuleOfSix&& other) noexcept;
};
```

See the following rule from the C++ Coding Guideline: C.21: If you define or =delete any copy, move, or destructor function, define or =delete them all[10].

---

[9]Thanks, JFT, for the suggestions on that!

[10]https://isocpp.github.io/CppCoreGuidelines/CppCoreGuidelines#c21-if-you-define-or-delete-any-copy-move-or-destructor-function-define-or-delete-them-all

Moveable-only types

```cpp
struct MoveableOnly {
    MoveableOnly() noexcept;
    ~MoveableOnly() noexcept;
    MoveableOnly(MoveableOnly&& other) noexcept;
    MoveableOnly& operator=(MoveableOnly&& other) noexcept;
};
```

In the above case, because we declare move operations, the compiler deletes copy operations:

```cpp
// MoveableOnly(const MoveableOnly&) = delete;
// MoveableOnly& operator=(const MoveableOnly&) = delete;
```

Example types: `std::unique_ptr`.

Polymorphic base classes

```cpp
struct BasePoly {
    virtual ~BasePoly() = default;
    BasePoly& operator=(BasePoly&& other) = delete;
    virtual void foo();
}
```

By declaring the move assignment, we prevent copy operations (they will be deleted); the move constructor is not declared. But we have to explicitly introduce a `virtual` destructor because, by default, the compiler creates only a non-virtual default destructor.

Appendix B - Quiz and Exercises Answers

See the correct answers:

The quiz from chapters 1...6

Q1: 2, as a side note, for classes with a base class, you can use inheriting constructors, which use a base class name, instead the derived class name to declare a constructor.

Q2: 2, Q3: 2, Q4: 3, Q5: 2, Q6: 2, 3,

Q7: 1, `auto` follows the rules of template type deduction, so references and constness are not preserved.

Q8: 1, 2, 3 - all answers are correct

Q9: 3 - since we have `auto elem : vec`, `elem` is a copy of an element from the vector, so if we change it, the value in the vector won't be affected.

Q10: 2, 3 - rvalue reference (42) can bind to a `const` reference or to a regular value.

The final quiz

Q1: 2, Q2: 2, Q3: 1, Q4: 1, Q5: 3, Q6: 2, Q7: 2, Q8: 1

Q9: 2, aggregates and in-class member initialization available since C++14

Q10: 2, (move constructor prevents implicit copy constructor, see code @C++Insights[11].

Q11: 2, the proper element type is `std::pair<const std::string, int>`, so each time, we'll have a copy in the loop iteration; see chapter on deduction.

Q12: 3, this is the special rule for the copy list initialization, it will yield `initializer_list`.

Q13: 1, a temporary is needed for `opt1`.

Q14: 3

Q15: 1, `initializer_list` requires a copyable type; see section "Some inconvenience - non-copyable types" in the non-regular data members chapter.

---

[11] https://cppinsights.io/s/9a1daa06

Solution to the first coding problem, NSDMI

Solution to the first coding problem. Run @Compiler Explorer

```cpp
struct Point { double x { 1.0 }; double y { 2.0 }; };
```

The solution uses NSDMI to initialize x and y to the required values.

Solution to the second coding problem, NSDMI

Solution to the second coding problem. Run @Compiler Explorer

```cpp
constexpr unsigned int DEFAULT_CATEGORY = 4;
constexpr unsigned int DEFAULT_FLAGS = 0x0a;
struct SalesRecord {
    std::string name_ {"empty"};
    double price_ { 1.0 };
    unsigned int category_ : 4 { DEFAULT_CATEGORY };
    unsigned int flags_ : 4 { DEFAULT_FLAGS};
};
```

The solution initializes data members to required values, including bit fields supported since C++20.

Solution to the third coding problem, `inline`

Solution to the Counted Type problem. Run @Wandbox

```cpp
struct CountedType {
    static inline int instanceCounter = 0;
    static inline int maxInstanceCounter = 0;

    // simple counting... only ctor and dtor implemented...
    CountedType() { ++instanceCounter; ++maxInstanceCounter; }
    ~CountedType() { --instanceCounter; }
    CountedType(const CountedType&) {
        ++instanceCounter; ++maxInstanceCounter;
    }
};
```

This solution implements a default constructor, a copy constructor, and a destructor. Since we want to know the maximum number of instances, this variable is not decremented in the destructor.

Solution to the fourth coding problem, fix code

Solution to the fourth problem. Run @Compiler Explorer

```cpp
struct SalesRec {
    std::string name_;
    double price_{}; // << make it 0 by default!
};
void addPromo(std::vector<SalesRec>& sales, double discount) {
    for (auto& elem : sales)            // << reference
        elem.price_ = (1.0-discount)*elem.price_;
}
double computeTotal(const std::vector<SalesRec>& sales) {
    double sum{}; // << set it to 0 at start
    for (const auto& elem : sales) // << don't copy elements
        sum += elem.price_;
    return sum;
}
```

The solution has 4 places with correct syntax. It forces `price_` and `sum` to be properly initialized to `0.0` at the start. Then it uses proper semantics for loop iterations.

References

Related materials and links about data member initialization in C++:

Proposals for C++ features:

- N2756[12] - Non-static data member initializers for C++11,
- P0683[13] - Default Bit Field Initializer for C++20,
- P0386[14] - Inline Variables C++17,
- P0329[15] - Designated Initializers C++20,
- P0960[16] and P1975[17] - Aggregate initialization from a parenthesized list for C++20.

Valuable resources for C++:

- C++ Standard Draft[18] - N4868 (October 2020 pre-virtual-plenary working draft/C++20 plus editorial changes),
- C++ compiler support - C++Reference[19] - a list of features and their compiler support since C++11,
- C++ Core Guidelines[20] - a community-edited and open guideline for C++ style, lead by Bjarne Stroustrup and Herb Sutter.

Books:

- "Embracing Modern C++ Safely"[21] by J. Lakos, V. Romeo, R. Khlebnikov, A. Meredith, a wonderful and very detailed book about latest C++ features, from C++11 till C++14 in the 1st edition.
- "Effective Modern C++: 42 Specific Ways to Improve Your Use of C++11 and C++14"[22] by Scott Meyers

---

[12]https://wg21.link/N2756
[13]https://wg21.link/P0683
[14]https://wg21.link/P0386
[15]https://wg21.link/P0329
[16]https://wg21.link/p0960
[17]https://wg21.link/p1975
[18]https://timsong-cpp.github.io/cppwp/n4868/
[19]https://en.cppreference.com/w/cpp/compiler_support
[20]https://isocpp.github.io/CppCoreGuidelines/CppCoreGuidelines
[21]https://amzn.to/3PywHTg
[22]https://amzn.to/3t5tmS4

Presentations:

- Core C++ 2019: Initialisation in modern C++[23] by Timur Doumler,
- CppCon 2018: "The Nightmare of Initialization in C"[24] by Nicolai Josuttis,
- CppCon 2021: Back To Basics: The Special Member Functions[25] by Klaus Iglberger,
- ACCU 2022: What Classes We Design and How[26] - by Peter Sommerlad,
- CppCon 2018 "The Bits Between the Bits: How We Get to main()"[27] - by Matt Godbolt.

Articles and other links:

- Non-Static Data Members Initialization - C++ Stories[28] - initial source for the book,
- What happens to your static variables at the start of the program? - C++ Stories[29],
- Always Almost Auto Style[30] by Herb Sutter,
- C++ Core Guidelines - C51[31] and C52[32] - about delegating and inheriting constructors,
- Modern C++ Features - Inherited and Delegating Constructors[33] by Arne Mertz,
- Trivial, standard-layout, POD, and literal types[34] at Microsoft Docs,
- Modern C++ Features - Uniform Initialization and initializer_list[35] by Arne Mertz,
- The cost of `std::initializer_list`[36] by Andrzej Krzemieński,
- Objects, their lifetimes and pointers[37] by Dawid Pilarski,
- Tutorial: When to Write Which Special Member[38] by Jonathan Müller,
- The implication of const or reference member variables in C++[39] by Lesley Lai,
- Brace initialization of user-defined types[40] by Glennan Carnie[41].

---

[23] https://www.youtube.com/watch?v=v0jM4wm1zYA
[24] https://www.youtube.com/watch?v=7DTlWPgX6zs
[25] https://www.youtube.com/watch?v=9BM5LAvNtus
[26] https://www.youtube.com/watch?v=fzsBZicBe88
[27] https://www.youtube.com/watch?v=dOfucXtyEsU
[28] https://www.cppstories.com/2015/02/non-static-data-members-initialization/
[29] https://www.cppstories.com/2018/02/staticvars/
[30] https://herbsutter.com/2013/08/12/gotw-94-solution-aaa-style-almost-always-auto/
[31] https://isocpp.github.io/CppCoreGuidelines/CppCoreGuidelines#c51-use-delegating-constructors-to-represent-common-actions-for-all-constructors-of-a-class
[32] https://isocpp.github.io/CppCoreGuidelines/CppCoreGuidelines#c52-use-inheriting-constructors-to-import-constructors-into-a-derived-class-that-does-not-need-further-explicit-initialization
[33] https://arne-mertz.de/2015/08/new-c-features-inherited-and-delegating-constructors/
[34] https://docs.microsoft.com/en-us/cpp/cpp/trivial-standard-layout-and-pod-types?view=msvc-170
[35] https://arne-mertz.de/2015/07/new-c-features-uniform-initialization-and-initializer_list/
[36] https://akrzemi1.wordpress.com/2016/07/07/the-cost-of-stdinitializer_list/
[37] https://blog.panicsoftware.com/objects-their-lifetimes-and-pointers/
[38] https://www.foonathan.net/2019/02/special-member-functions/
[39] https://lesleylai.info/en/const-and-reference-member-variables/
[40] https://blog.feabhas.com/2019/04/brace-initialization-of-user-defined-types/
[41] https://blog.feabhas.com/author/glennan/

Index

Symbols
&& - see rvalue
& - see reference
= - see assignment operator
[[attr]] - see attributes
{...} - see curly braces
(...) - see parens
[x, y] - see structured binding

A
AAA, Almost Always Auto 110
API 3, 13
accumulate, std:: 13, 14
aggregate initialization 8, 207-217
array, std::
　aggregates 208
　containers 139-141
　CTAD 107
　NSDMI 124, 125
　other 1, 39, 43, 208, 239, 240
assignment operator, copy 55, 62, 134 232
assignment operator, move 55, 62, 159, 170
attributes 17, 104
auto type deduction 24, 94, 125
automatic storage duration 6, 87, 177

B
begin, std:: 108
bit field 131
braces, curly 22, 92, 133, 200, 202
brace elision 209

C
C++ Core Guidelines
　classes 14, 15, 35, 53, 71, 85
　initialization, 24, 137
　memory 80
　other 86, 182
C++ Reference page 269
C++ Insights 47, 89, 143, 173, 204
chrono, std:: 110, 260
CTAD 91, 107, 108, 133, 137, 208, 240
Compiler Explorer V, most examples
Compiler-generated 28, 40, 45, 54, 89, 137, 138
closure 92, 95, 113
Clang 52, 158, 210, 215, 225
Clang-tidy 226
const
　deduction 94-99, 103-106, 108, 111
　initializer_list, 142-155
　members 157-159, 171
　other 14, 22, 30, 39, 41, 48, 63, 64, 92, 181, 223
constant, initialization 2, 188, 189, 190, 191, 205
constexpr 17, 26, 106, 178, 188, 190, 191, 204, 247
constructor
　default 5, 17-22, 27-30, 60-64, 137-140, 158, 231
　copy 31, 39-64, 127-129, 158, 241, 260
　converting 33, 36-38
　move 39, 47-64, 127-130, 163, 170, 234, 260
　explicit 18, 31, 34, 37, 219
containers
　aggregates 230
　as members 139 - 155
　other 8, 24, 25, 41, 51, 80, 90, 96, 112
conversion 2, 32, 33, 34, 36, 37, 38, 92, 111, 211
copy and swap idiom 60, 219, 232, 234
copy elision 2, 44, 45, 112, 247
copy initialization
　basics 2, 7, 10, 11, 124, 136, 141, 221
　conversion 36

deduction 94, 95, 107, 112
differences 34
operations 42
curly braces 6, 22, 24, 60, 140, 211, 214
cv-qualifiers 38, 94, 99

D
data members
  static 5, 60, 134, 177, 188, 194, 203
  non-static 19, 45, 54, 104, 119-138, 176, 214
declaration 3
decltype 91
deep copy 40
default initialization 2, 5, 10, 125, 136, 141, 150
default, constructor, see constructor
definition 3
delegating constructor 66
delete, = 17, 30, 260, 263
delete, operator 75, 78
designated initializers 207, 213, 214, 238
destructor 26, 46, 54 62, 75
direct list initialization 21, 39, 94, 124

E
elision
  brace 209, 210
  copy 44, 45, 112
emplace 51, 219, 227, 230
emplace_back 150, 152, 153, 212, 240
end, std:: 108, 142
exceptions 24, 25, 50, 86, 88, 233
extern 3, 6, 177, 178, 179, 182, 204

F
-fno-elide-constructors 44, 193
factory function 242
Fluent C++, blog 23, 204, 222, 237
for-loop 92, 105, 108-112, 142
forward, std:: 154, 231

G
GCC 20, 35, 44, 52, 68, 159, 166, 193, 210, 215
getters 59, 119
global variables 177, 178, 180, 182, 188, 190, 203
Google C++ Style 14, 113

H
heap 2, 75, 78, 79, 166
header file 137, 167, 197, 201-204

I
in_place_t 228-232, 252
indeterminate values 5, 6, 11, 20, 29, 234
inheritance 15, 18, 64, 65, 68, 69, 71, 82, 261
inheriting constructor 65, 68, 71, 72
initialization
  aggregate 8, 212, 198
  constant 188-191, 205
  default 2, 5, 10, 125, 136, 141, 150
  definition, 1
  direct 2, 7, 10, 21, 24, 34, 39, 124, 135, 141, 211
  copy, see copy initialization
  list 8, 21-24, 94, 137, 140, 142
  reference 2
  value 6-11, 15, 16, 28, 63, 124
  zero 2, 11, 64, 188
initializer_list 24, 95, 101, 135, 141-155, 230
inline, variable 127, 196, 198-205, 234
iterator 91, 102, 105, 108, 142, 144

J
join(), thread 184
jthread, std:: 183-185, 193

L
Lifetime extension 108, 143
Logging 18, 25, 26, 42, 58-60, 228
lambda 92, 95, 106, 113, 172, 173
lifetime 75-77, 109, 143, 162, 168, 177, 185, 195
limitations 67, 106, 132, 133, 137, 211

linkage
    external 178-, 179, 182, 195
    module 178
    internal 178, 180-182
    no/empty 178, 179
    language 178
local variable 1, 179, 184-186, 192, 242

M
MSVC 52,
make_optional, std:: 230, 231
make_unique, std:: 79, 83, 88, 110, 212, 243, 246
map, std:: 90-92, 105, 139, 140, 141, 145, 184, 244
member initialization list 41, 122
memory leak 78, 86-88
move, std:: 48-52, 130, 146, 164, 223-225
moveable-only types 157, 264
mutable, 26, 34
mutex, std:: 107, 112, 157, 183, 229
narrowing conversion 32, 33, 211

N
NRVO 44
NSDMI 10, 119-138, 141, 159, 234, 238, 253, 255
new, operator 107, 186
noexcept 14, 17, 29, 50-53, 56-59, 89, 130, 233
non-local 2, 6, 177, 186, 187, 188
non-regular 157
nullptr 161, 170, 188, 243, 245
nullptr_t, std:: 94

O
operator
    overloading 54
    new, 107, 186
    delete 119
    assignment 39, 54-64, 159-163, 170,176, 230
optimization 40, 44, 45, 48, 50, 52
optional, std:: 36, 227-232
ownership 48, 79, 164

P
pair, std:: 92, 102, 134, 191
parens 124, 135-137, 140-146, 211-214, 217
partially created 85, 87, 88
perfect forwarding 154, 231
pimpl pattern 161, 162, 166
POD 64, 105
polymorphism 82, 84, 236
PRETTY_FUNCTION 100
prvalue 38, 93, 98

Q
qualifiers, cv 94, 99
qualifiers, ref 97, 98

R
RAII 90, 186, 187
random number generator 186
range based for loop
raw pointer 86, 160, 161, 163, 165, 166, 170, 174
reference, as members 171
reference_wrapper, std:: 173, 174
regular, type 155
resource 40, 48, 73, 86-88, 163, 164, 168, 170, 187
rule of five or six 263
rule of three 262
rule of zero 262
rvalue 14, 92, 96, 154, 223

S
security 5, 6
setters 59, 119
shallow copy 40, 163, 170
shared_ptr, std:: 79, 168, 169, 170
singleton 193, 219, 241, 242
smart pointer 79, 81, 84, 88, 163, 165, 170, 186
span, std:: 161
special member function
    constructors 13, 16, 39, 157, 162-166, 168
    destructors 75, 76, 89
    trivial 60, 62

rules 259
standard layout 64
static initialization 187, 188, 189, 190, 204, 242
static order init fiasco 188, 189, 190, 204
storage duration
    automatic 5, 6, 87, 177, 179
    static 179, 181, 195, 247
    thread, 177, 182
    dynamic 186
string_view, std:: 100, 125, 161, 226
string literal 22, 110, 152, 166, 223
strong types 219, 220, 221, 222
structured binding 102, 104, 105, 106
swap, std:: 233

T

template 97-100, 106-108, 133, 134, 153, 230, 235
temporary 22, 45-50, 75, 93, 104-110, 150, 225
terminate(), std:: 50, 86
thread, std:: 174, 183-185, 193
thread_local 6, 177, 182-185
throw 25, 65, 85, 87, 88
trivial types 26, 63, 64, 191, 204
translation unit 3, 178-182, 188, 198-199, 204
tuple, std:: 104, 108, 154
type deduction 1, 24, 91-113, 124, 132
type traits 175

U

UB, see undefined behaviour
undefined behavior 5-6, 11, 109
union 31, 188
unique_ptr, std:: 79, 83, 88, 124, 152-154, 164-168, 186
universal reference 97, 154
user-provided 6, 31, 60-63
user-defined literals 222

V

value initialization 2, 6-9, 10, 15, 16, 28, 63, 124
value categories 93
variadic function 153,

variant, std:: 227, 231, 232
vector, std:: 41, 50, 109, 134, 141, 147-154, 212
vexing parse 22, 23, 136
virtual, function 8, 62, 63, 71, 82, 84, 207

W

worker, thread 183, 185, 193
wrapper 36, 80, 160-168, 173, 219, 227, 237

Z

zero initialization 2, 64, 188

www.ingramcontent.com/pod-product-compliance
Lightning Source LLC
Chambersburg PA
CBHW080451220526
45465CB00006B/2232